THE
KIPPER PATROL

THE
KIPPER PATROL

The History of 608 (NR) Squadron Royal Auxiliary Air Force
and Thornaby Aerodrome 1930-1957

Louise Wilkinson

PNEUMA SPRINGS PUBLISHING UK

First Published 2009
Published by Pneuma Springs Publishing

The Kipper Patrol
Copyright © 2009 Louise Wilkinson
ISBN: 978-1-905809-45-5

Cover design, editing and typesetting by:
Pneuma Springs Publishing

A Subsidiary of Pneuma Springs Ltd.
7 Groveherst Road, Dartford Kent, DA1 5JD.
E: admin@pneumasprings.co.uk
W: www.pneumasprings.co.uk

A catalogue record for this book is available from the
British Library.

For my Dad, Frank Wilkinson, who never lived to see this finished, but who would have been so proud. I love you.

And for the young, Amy, Alice, Josh, Daniel, Mikey and Neve. I am so proud of you all. Be happy.

CONTENTS

ACKNOWLEDGEMENTS

608 Squadron Royal Auxiliary Air Force were formed on 17th March 1930, and whilst this book will put forward their history, it is very difficult to separate their history from the history of Thornaby Aerodrome itself, since the two are intrinsically linked and grew up together. Since 608 Squadron was the local Auxiliary squadron its base, for most of its existence was Thornaby Aerodrome, although the squadron did move to other areas of the country, in particular Wick in Scotland and then overseas during World War Two. Thus it is apparent that the two histories overlap in such a way that the story of the two should be told together in one book.

I should also mention that I didn't want to write a book about aircraft, although the different aircraft did play a vital role within both the squadron and the aerodrome. I wanted to write a book about the men and the day to day life of the aerodrome, which is based upon interviews that I have conducted with many veterans from the squadron and their families. The photographs and memories that they have shared with me I now feel privileged to share with you.

As a local history teacher, I was fascinated by the idea that less than a hundred years ago, there was an aerodrome at Thornaby, with men flying in and out, and personnel using local amenities and helping the area economically. I was also interested in the idea that the main squadron to be based at Thornaby throughout the period 1930-1957 was an auxiliary squadron. Effectively this meant that it was a reserve or part-time squadron, a squadron made up of local men who joined the Auxiliary Air Force as a way to work with and fly planes in their spare time. This was interesting because it meant that the men who joined the squadron had made a conscious decision to be a part of the AAF and had an interest in being a member of a voluntary organisation where men from different backgrounds mixed together in the work place.

Many of the men who I have interviewed said that "the auxiliary air force was a 'gentleman's' flying club" made up of young men from wealthy backgrounds who used the organisation as a way to allow them to fly. Was this true? Perhaps not, but it was an interesting area to research and that is how my interest in 608 Squadron and Thornaby Aerodrome began.

After reading widely on mid-20th century Britain, covering topics such as, the history of the Royal Air Force, local air-fields, local history, class issues, social history of the mid-20th century and inter-war policy on rearmament, my ideas were shaped and reshaped by the information that I read. Yet factual information on the formation, development and history of 608 Squadron and Thornaby Aerodrome was very limited. I visited the National Archives at Kew in London on several occasions as I searched for information to answer my growing questions. The operational record books of Thornaby Aerodrome and of 608 Squadron contained day-by-day accounts of the running of the station and the squadron, the staff, the planes, the missions flown, the accidents and the deaths. This factual information helped me to piece together what life would have been like on an RAF Station. Finally the documents held at the National Archives helped me to understand how and why the Auxiliary Air Force was created, what its role was, and why the decision was taken to disband it in 1957.

Through Sandra Harper, the schools press officer, I put out press releases asking for anyone who served in 608 Squadron, or who had been stationed at Thornaby Aerodrome, who would be prepared to talk about their experiences, to contact me. I was amazed at the response. Men and women, both young and old contacted me, and so I embarked on a series of interviews which have helped me to write my thesis, submitted in September 2008, which has a working title of "Gentleman's flying club to technical meritocracy – 608 Squadron and the Auxiliary Air Force 1930-1957." This book is the result of my research and a promise that I made to the veterans who have helped me to learn about both the squadron and the station, without their support, neither would have been possible.

There are several people who deserve personal thanks:

John Pollock, one of the veterans of 608 Squadron worked for many hours helping me find photographs and information on other veterans from the squadron. I am now proud to call him my friend.

The staff and pupils of Grangefield School, Stockton on Tees, for their understanding and interest during my six years of study and research. In particular I must mention my friends, Helen Beadnall who helped to keep me sane when I was "a woman on the edge" and Stuart Arthur who gave up his time to research the backgrounds of a couple of the more elusive 1930s officers from 608 Squadron.

Special thanks go to the school librarian Lol O'Donnell who helped me so much typing up and re-organising my thesis bibliography, and working on the thankless task of the contents pages, bibliography and index of this book. She is a superstar!!

My close friend Joan Covell, who in her younger days had attended many of the 608 Squadron dances and her husband Fred, and also their daughter Sue, who ran round Thornaby handing out my "request for information" posters.

Finally personal thanks go to my mum, Kathleen Wilkinson, who read my thesis, searched for obituaries in her newspaper and paid my university fees far too many times.

Most of all, this is for Pam, Lyndsey and Kerrianne who have put up with never seeing me, and trying to pretend that they were interested in what I was talking about.

Thank you all. It's finished now!!!!!

List of Illustrations

Introduction

To begin then, some background information on the history of flight. In 1909, Louis Bleriot became the first man to fly across the English Channel, and David Lloyd George, Chancellor of the Exchequer stated, "Flying machines are no longer toys and dreams, they are established fact. The possibilities of this new system of locomotion are infinite. Britain is no longer an island." For centuries Britain had relied upon its island status to keep it safe. As an Imperial power, Britain was also required to protect its Empire and its trade routes. However, there was now a potential threat from a military point of view. There was much internal debate within both the Royal Navy and the Army as to the place of aviation in future military developments, temporarily settled in 1911, when a Sub-Committee of Imperial Defence, chaired by Lord Haldane, recommended the creation of the Royal Flying Corps, which was to consist of a Naval wing, a Military wing and a Central Flying School. Thus, this new military flying organisation was not a separate entity, nor was it a third service, but rather an extension to the existing military network. As the war progressed, and the usefulness of aviation in terms of its military purpose began to be recognised, a Cabinet Committee was formed under General Jan Smuts, he recommended the creation of a separate Air Ministry with a statement "the day may not be far off when aerial operations with their devastation of enemy lands and destruction of industries and populous centres on a vast scale may become the principal operations of the war, to which older forms of military and naval operations may become secondary and subordinate." Smut's report was not well received by either the army or the navy with both sides opposing the creation of a third military force, after all, this could lead to a reduction in funding for each of them. The Government, however, followed Smuts and on 1st April 1918, the Royal Flying Corps and the Royal Naval Air Service were merged to form the Royal Air Force.

The inter-war period proved to be the testing ground for the RAF. In November 1919, Hugh Trenchard became Chief of the Air Staff. He understood the need to raise the profile of the infant RAF highlighting the potential role in policing the British Empire, thus reducing the cost of staffing large garrisons overseas. He also set up a part-time reserve force, along similar lines to the Territorial Army. This meant that a pool of trained pilots and airmen would be created who could slip into full time service if the need arose. Volunteers were committed to learning about the organisation that they spent their free time with; they were enthusiastic and prepared to work together as part of a team for the good of the country. In this way, voluntarism and patriotism could be linked together to benefit the country as a whole. Under the Air Force Constitution Act of 1917, there was provision for two different types of reserve forces, the Auxiliary Air Force and the Special Reserve.

By creating two institutions that were separate but similar, they could provide as broad a basis as possible for recruitment and would also offer a wider national appeal. A significant difference however was that although the Territorial Army and the AAF were administered by the county associations, the Special Reserve squadrons were to be a part of the Royal Air Force proper, and were administered and funded by them. This reflected the uncertainty and conflict between government officials over the creation, funding and administration of a reserve air force and the idea was shelved for three years due largely to the attitude of the country as a whole towards military expenditure during the interwar years and the fact that there was a major economic and financial crisis. In fact, the winter of 1920-21 saw the end of the post war economic boom brought about by large reductions in government spending, an increase of taxation and the failure to increase British exports. Coupled with increased overproduction there was a decline in demand for coal and textiles resulting in a massive rise in unemployment. The government blamed public expenditure and appointed Sir Edward Geddes to chair the committee on National Expenditure, the final report, published in February 1922, became known as the Geddes Axe, a sweeping round of public service cuts specifically in the army, navy, education and public health. It was in this political climate that Trenchard began to lobby for the new reserve forces to be created. However, concerns were raised about whether "air crew, and especially pilots, could achieve and retain proficiency in the air as a part-time and mainly weekend activity."

By mid 1923 discussions were once again taking place regarding the formation of Special Reserve and Auxiliary Air Force squadrons. It was considered necessary to form two separate organisations so that the conditions of service for the reserve provided for enlistment on as broad a basis as possible. Furthermore, there was an element of competition built in and one might assume, also a recognition that one or other organisation was on borrowed time. Subsequently, the idea was that "the most efficient and economical method of administration could only be ascertained by experience and two separate forces would provide a wider national appeal. In addition, it might be necessary to expand to a large number of squadrons in either or both forces which ever proved by experience to be the more efficient and popular form or organisation."

Furthermore there was clearly disagreement about how the AAF would work as well as how much it would cost the Government. Judging from preliminary talks regarding the creation of two different types of reserve forces it would appear that the S R squadrons were in direct competition with the AAF squadrons from the start. Moreover, advocates of an RAF reserve clearly looked to the army as a baseline. Thus Samuel Hoare, Secretary of State for Air, and one of the staunch advocates of the AAF stated "the Special Reserve squadrons were intended to be 'formed on a militia basis' whereas the Auxiliary Air Force would be 'formed more nearly on a territorial basis.'"

Overall, the idea was that SR squadrons would attract people to whom a closer connection with the life of the regular air force appealed, while AAF squadrons envisaged the recruitment of officers and men who wished to serve together on a more local and amateur basis. Thus, following a number of false starts and protracted debate in 1924, the Auxiliary Air Force and Air Forces Reserve Act was passed. This allowed for six Auxiliary squadrons and seven Special Reserve squadrons, the eventual aim being twenty Auxiliary squadrons in total.

Contemporary notes regarding the formation of SR and AAF squadrons highlight the main differences between the two types of squadrons. With regard to the Special Reserve squadrons, officers and men were to be recruited direct by the units, officers were taught to fly in the units, airmen had to be skilled tradesmen and were enlisted in their trades, and the squadrons were formed near centres of engineering population. The Auxiliary Air Force on the other hand recruited both officers and airmen through the local Territorial and AAF associations, officers were not accepted unless they could already fly and on acceptance the cost of training was refunded, airmen need not be skilled tradesmen because they were taught their trades in the units and squadrons were formed near large towns and had town headquarters where training was carried on throughout the year culminating in an annual camp. This meant that the SR squadrons would be reliant on up to two thirds of its personnel living in the neighbourhood of the aerodrome. These conditions would be made as elastic as possible to minimise interference with the civil life of officers and airmen.

Thus the idea was to supplement the regular Royal Air Force personnel with additional volunteers who lived close to an existing operational aerodrome and who were able to reinforce the skills required. These conditions of service were different from those of the Auxiliary Air Force which was to be raised and maintained by the County Territorial Associations and manned by locally recruited non-regular personnel, with only a small core of regulars as permanent staff. The clear differences between the Special Reserves and the Auxiliary Air Force as James has noted was that the AAF "resembled much more closely the old Yeomanry regiments."

By 1931 members of the RAF Establishment Committee began to consider their options with regard to personnel in the future, and the idea began to be floated of merging the SR squadrons into the AAF. The arguments put forward were that, in favour of the merger, there would be a greater economy of personnel, since there were fewer regulars in the AAF and consequently it was less expensive to run. There would also be a greater ease in recruiting men, because choice would be limited to one rather than two organisations and also there were fewer constraints on entry in the AAF than in the SR. This would mean that those who wanted to become members of the RAF volunteers would know exactly what they were volunteering for and what was required of them, rather than having to look at two different sets of rules, regulations and opportunities. This is in fact the exact opposite of the original thinking with regard to a Territorial Air Force. Another reason given for the merger was the possibility of higher professional standards, because recruiting procedures would be adhered to strictly due to the lack of choice available. Moreover, the unit belonged to the volunteers and there was likely to be a greater *e'spirit* de corps if the men were largely reserves as opposed to being largely regulars with a smaller number of volunteers. Finally there was the idea of civic voluntarism because an AAF unit, fostered by the town or country, would have much more local influence and atmosphere than a regular squadron because the men would all have dual roles in both the local community and as part of the squadron as a whole. Between 1935 and 1937 the Special Reserve squadrons, whose numbers were located in the 500 series, were merged into the Auxiliary Air Force.

However, as the need to recruit more reserve pilots increased, it became clear that since the Auxiliary Air Force was something of a *corps d'elite* and was composed of formed units, it was an unsuitable organisation to handle the vast number of reserve pilots who had to be recruited and trained. The idea of a Volunteer Reserve was developed in 1936. Broadly the aim was to train 800 pilots a year in an organisation based not on the County Associations but on Town Centres situated in industrial areas. The necessary sites were acquired, the contracts with civil flying firms concluded, and the Royal Air Force Volunteer Reserve came into being in April 1937." Its purpose was to fill the gaps between the entry requirements of the Auxiliary Air Force and the regular RAF, "the intention was to convey a clear message that whilst there was an educational hurdle to be surmounted there were to be no social barriers for reservists to cross."

Thus, the RAFVR would have a wider appeal to potential pilot recruits and would ensure that background and status did not become an obstacle for enlistment, as perceived to be the case in the AAF. Air Chief Marshall, Lord Tedder, intended that the RAFVR should not be connected to the County Associations to whom the AAF was connected and largely controlled. He intended to recruit from a wide range, including poorer secondary school boys as well as boys from the more expensive public schools, since these young men from contrasting social backgrounds would have to be able to work together both in the air and on the ground. A common pre-war anecdote pointed out that "auxiliaries are gentlemen trying to be officers; regulars are officers trying to be gentlemen; V.R's are neither trying to be both. Subsequently the idea was that the RAFVR would be more accessible to local people because regulations surrounding entry were less rigid. Members of the RAFVR did not need to be officers to fly, and it also allowed men without a trade to become serving members enabling them to train on entry. The decision to create the RAFVR was significant since "in January 1938 the AAF was running at only 51% of its peacetime establishment of pilots and following a committee of enquiry chaired by Under Secretary of State, Harold Balfour, it was forced to begin – in the face of opposition from amongst its squadrons – to train some of its own non-commissioned ground and aircrew members as pilots to compensate for the shortfall of its officer numbers. Even so, it entered the war still seriously below its established strength." By 1939, there were approximately five thousand RAFVR pilots.

The Local Area

The main focus for Teesside and the Tees Valley is the River Tees, whose source is in the North Pennines at Tees Head. During the seventeenth and eighteenth centuries, industry and commerce on the River Tees were still in their early stages. In the Victorian Age industry boomed and gave Teesside a common industrial heritage, which unified the North and South banks of the river. Stockton began as an Anglo Saxon settlement located on high ground close to the northern banks of the River Tees. By the seventeenth century, it was beginning to take over Yarm's role as the main port on the River Tees. It was however, still largely an agricultural area and this is shown by the fact that the main goods exported from Stockton were local agricultural produce and lead from Durham.

Together with the expansion of coal production in South Durham and the opening of the Stockton and Darlington railway in 1825, there were significant increases in trade and population for the town. However, the extension of the railway line to Middlesbrough in 1830 effectively ended the use of Stockton as a port because Middlesbrough was located six miles closer to the sea. Furthermore, Middlesbrough was a newer town, created in 1829 when a group of Quaker businessmen headed by Joseph Pease of Darlington purchased a farmstead and its estate and set about developing it. By 1830 the Stockton and Darlington railway line had been extended to Middlesbrough making the rapid expansion of the town and port inevitable. Within twenty years Middlesbrough's population had risen to 7,600 and Middlesbrough was rapidly replacing Stockton as the main port on the River Tees.

In 1850, iron ore was discovered in the Cleveland Hills and slowly it began to replace coal as the main industry of the area. Iron was in big demand in Britain, specifically due to the rapid expansion of railways. More and more blast furnaces opened to meet the demand and this meant that by the end of the century, Teesside was producing one third of the country's output of iron.

By 1870, steel, a much stronger and more resilient metal was being produced at the Bessemer Steel Plant in Middlesbrough, the steel being used for bridge construction by Dorman Long who built the Newport lifting bridge, which opened in February 1934. Furthermore, metal making was the dominant industry within the economy of Middlesbrough employing hundreds of workers. By the turn of the century, the population of Middlesbrough had risen to 90,000. The development of the steel industry occurred alongside technological improvements, which led to Teesside becoming the world centre for steel growth - the Sydney Harbour Bridge and the Tyne Bridge were both made from Teesside steel. But the industry suffered badly during the depression, which created a tremendous shock for managers and employees. It was probably the start of the end for the steel industry on Teesside. In addition, Teesside had experienced high levels of immigration into the area, among them a group of Irish Catholics and highly specialised workers from Wales. This created an increase in the local population and further increased the unemployment figures for the region.

Thornaby is located on the southern banks of the River Tees with Stockton across the river on the north bank and Middlesbrough to the East. The Victorian town centre was developed in the nineteenth century around the banks of the River Tees. Stockton grew with the establishment of shipbuilding and engineering in the area and gradually South Stockton swallowed up the small village of Thornaby so that on 6th October 1892 the two areas merged to form the Municipal Borough of Thornaby on Tees.

Industry in the Thornaby area consisted in the main of Head Wrightson (Teesdale) Ltd, formed in 1860 by engineer Thomas Wrightson who teamed up with the Teesside engineering company Head Ashby and Co, a Thornaby foundry started in 1840. They were involved in the war effort by building landing craft for the D-Day landings despite suffering bomb damage from German air raids. Other industry in the area included the North Yorkshire Ironworks founded on April 5th 1865 by Richardson Johnson and Co. This company changed its name to A Bainbridge and made angular, railway and iron bars, it also had a brickworks. The Bon Lea Foundry was founded in 1848 as a works for making gas, water and drain pipes and in 1936 the company joined Federated Foundries Ltd.

R J Crosthwaite was founded in 1875 and joined Allied Iron Founders in 1928. It produced cast iron pipes and fittings. Mr R W Crosthwaite whose son owned Thornaby Hall established this company. There was also the Erimus Ironworks. There were other industries in Thornaby that did not involve iron making, for example, Appleton French and Co who made flour, John I Hopper Ltd who made wire ropes, W & M Pumphrey Ltd who were food processors and North Eastern Breweries Ltd.

The other principle employer in the Teesside area was ICI, which was set up in December 1926 following the merger of four chemical companies. After World War II ICI began a huge expansion of the chemical industry on Teesside with the development of a site at Wilton, at the height of production, the Billingham plant employed 16,000 people and the Wilton site, 20,000. The ICI plant at Billingham was heavily involved in the production of high performance aviation fuel for the Royal Air Force during World War II. From 1934 onwards, Billingham ICI also became a centre for plastics production and many of the products were used during the Second World War in the construction of aircraft cockpits. During World War II the ICI sites at Billingham and Wilton were heavily camouflaged to protect them from potential bombing.

Apart from the major employers there were also lots of local family businesses around the area, Vaux Breweries, Newhouse's stores, Shaw's Foundry at Ormesby, to name but a few. These family businesses employed much smaller numbers of staff. Industry on Teesside provided the environment through which men could learn skills that would be mutually beneficial. The Depression in the 1930s meant that unemployment became a significant problem in the Teesside area and meant that recruitment into the Auxiliary Air Force may have had a wider appeal because it offered men the opportunity to utilise their skills and earn extra money to supplement their incomes.

In terms of leisure opportunities for Teesside, municipal leisure facilities such as public parks, libraries and swimming pools were enjoyed by the local population, supplemented by modern commercial leisure facilities, for example, public houses including the Odd Fellows, the Jolly Farmers, the Cleveland, the Half Moon and the New Inn, cinemas such as the Queens, the Central and the Mayfair located in Thornaby, and dance halls in Stockton such as the Palais, the Jubilee and the Maison de Dance. The developments in transport over the period and the improvement in roads allowed towns to be linked together by vehicles such as buses, trams and to a certain extent, cars and motorbikes. The proximity of Thornaby Aerodrome to the local amenities enabled both officers and airmen to socialise outside of the Station if they wanted to.

To summarise, the importance of the iron and steel making industries to the local economy was significant prior to the Second World War. Since Teesside was an area which contained a large number of skilled workers, several immigrants and a high percentage of unemployed workers. It was the close proximity of Teesside to local industry, which made Thornaby a suitable choice by the Air Ministry for the location of an aerodrome, which would become an RAF station in the late 1930s and an important Coastal Command post throughout the Second World War.

The 1930s

The first flying over Thornaby took place on Thursday 26th July 1912, when Mr Gustav Hamel, one of the early aviators who was taking part in the Daily Mail Newspapers "Circuit of Britain" event, provided a flying display to some 12,000 people at the Durham County Show which was held in Stockton. Mr Hamel then returned to Thornaby on Saturday 28 July 1912 when he flew from Redcar to a field on the Vale Farm belonging to Mr Matthew Young. Between 5,000 and 6,000 people paid for admission to the field whilst the adjacent roadway for a mile or more was densely packed with sightseers. Mr Hamel approached the field at a rapid speed at about 3.30 and before descending; he delighted the spectators, many of whom were seeing an aeroplane for the first time, with a daring exhibition of volpaning (gliding toward the earth with the engine off) and banking, finally landing following a corkscrew volpane. Mr Hamel was welcomed by the Mayor of Thornaby, Colonel G O Spence and others, including Alderman and Mrs O A Head. Hamel's Bleriot Monoplane was wheeled around the arena in order that everyone might have a good view of it and, after about an hour, Mr Hamel again took his seat and after encircling the aerodrome once or twice, rose to a height of around 2,400 feet and disappeared in the direction of the mouth of the Tees.

The next move towards aviation in Thornaby took place in 1925 when the Air Ministry began negotiations for the opening of a full time airfield at Thornaby. The aerodrome was constructed on land that had originally belonged to the Crosthwaite family who lived at Thornaby Hall. Fifty acres of land had also been bought from Thornaby Grange, The Vale Farm, Thornaby Lodge Farm, Franklands Farm at Stainsby and Harry Foggin. The airfield at Thornaby opened officially on 29th September 1929.

The local squadron, No 608 Squadron Auxiliary Air Force was formed on 17th March 1930 with a squadron strength of one officer and eleven airmen. At that time the hanger and various buildings were still in the process of being built. Recruitment was stepped up, but was hampered for two reasons, firstly the lack of proper accommodation for the airmen, and secondly the fact that the local Territorial and Auxiliary Forces Association were unable to offer the Squadron more than fifty pounds to be used for recruitment. Local employers and family businesses were keen to support volunteers for the AAF because it was seen to be putting something back into the community. Families had pride in their son's commitment to their country and to their local area. It was a time of patriotism, when the country and its status in the world was important, and men were prepared to give up their free time, supported by their families and employers, to give something back. On 7th May 1930 608 Squadron received its first aircraft, an Avro Lynx.

The North Eastern Daily Gazette reported in 1930, that "every effort was being made to make the aerodrome the largest and best in the country. There would be twenty-four service planes and opportunity would be afforded for training in engineering, aeroplane rigging, photography, gunnery and bombing. Local craftsmen would be trained for the various jobs after they had joined the squadron, which would virtually mean the establishment of a new industry for the district." Recruiting took place from December 1930 to bring the squadron up to establishment strength, but the press noted that "difficulties with recruiting could be because it rather looks as if there were some difficulty about getting officer personnel of the right calibre to join these squadrons or as if they could not get enough other ranks to join and so flying personnel could not be appointed."

The first Commanding Officer of 608 Squadron was Squadron Leader W Howard Davies, the son of RW and JP Howard Davis of Elton House, Darlington. He lived in Saltburn and worked as Chief Accountant to Dorman Long. He was appointed to command the squadron on 16th June 1930. The first hanger was completed on 24th July 1930, and Geoffrey Shaw was commissioned as a Pilot Officer. In October Ivo Thompson was commissioned as a Pilot Officer and shortly after the new airmen's barrack block was completed. At that time the squadron establishment was three officers and 32 other ranks. In the early months of 1931 several other young men received their commissions as Pilot Officers, these included Geoffrey Ambler, A N Wilson, Keith Pyman, C W Wright and H C Newhouse.

Recruiting of auxiliary airmen was stepped up but was hampered by the lack of proper accommodation. By July 1931 the Squadron consisted of eight officers and thirty-eight auxiliary airmen. The press pointed out on that occasion the aerodrome adjoined the village of old Thornaby. It was one of the most spacious Auxiliary Air Force stations in the county, and occupied 200 acres, commanding to the southeast a splendid view of the Cleveland Hills. Thornaby Hall made a delightful officer's mess.

John Pollock's Collection

The barracks block was nearing completion, while a combined drill hall and institute was to be erected together with an armoury, photographic section and motor transport shed. The airmen were enlisted as Air Crafts Men Second Class and underwent training in whichever trade they wished to take up, the period of enlistment being four years. During the summer, weekend camps would be held, and the auxiliary airmen would go under canvas.

Mr G Davies Collection

The officers were given instructions in flying on both training and service types of aircraft and in addition received instruction on a variety of different subjects. Clearly the lack of complete accommodation for both aeroplanes and personnel was causing problems for the recruiting of more staff to bring the squadron up to its establishment strength, however those men who were already enlisted as members of 608 squadron AAF were committed, keen and enthusiastic.

By early 1930 the road leading to Thornaby Hall had been widened and a corrugated iron aeroplane shed, watch hut and various brick buildings were erected. The new airman's barrack block was completed on 1st November 1930. The North Eastern Daily Gazette noted in March 1931 "the airport at Thornaby is now a year old. In a huge hanger, screened from the road and inquisite public gaze are housed half-a-dozen aeroplanes of the lighter classes, whilst the strength of the RAF detachment is 32. Every evening members of the Territorial detachments report here for instruction, and at weekends, when they come in the afternoon, the theory they have learned during the week is demonstrated practically." This story was also picked up by the Yorkshire Daily Herald who noted that "Yorkshire's only air squadron celebrated their first birthday. Outwardly there was no sign that the day was any different from any other. In the evening the commanding officer Squadron Leader W Howard Davies entertained a number of guests in the officer's mess, including Colonel Arthur Godman, air representative on the North Riding Territorial Association." It is clear from the newspaper reports which are found in the 608 Squadron scrap-book, that the press were very interested in the exploits of 608 Squadron throughout the 1930s and were very proud of the local men who were members of the squadron. The completion of accommodation for the Auxiliary Squadron of the Royal Air Force – No 608 (Bombing) Squadron stationed at Thornaby, was to cost the sum of £87,000 when completed by March 1934. Training of auxiliaries had begun in January 1931 and there were 11 officers and 65 airmen, as opposed to the permanent staff of 3 officers and 40 other ranks.

The first weekend camp held by 608 Squadron took place in July 1931, and was honoured by a visit from Sir Hugh Bell, the Lord-Lieutenant of the North Riding and President of the North Riding Territorial Association. A demonstration of formation flying and acrobatics was given for the visitors. The squadron strength was noted as eight officers and thirty-eight auxiliary airmen. Squadron aircraft were two Westland Wapiti's, five Avro's and two Moths. Sir Hugh Bell commented on "the great enthusiasm and keenness with which the training is carried out by the Auxiliary Pilot Officers, and the Auxiliary Airmen, and he congratulated Squadron Leader Howard Davies on the progress made in the formation and training of the unit.

Sunday 16th August 1931 saw 608 Squadron holding a tea party as part of its annual two week summer camp. Visitors were invited to watch a flying exhibition in blinding rain, lightening and heavy thunder. Nine machines took to the air to perform a one hour display, two groups of three aircraft displayed perfect flying formation flying whilst the remaining three aircraft performed thrilling aerobatics. Spectators watched the display from inside the large hanger. The squadron strength was noted to be 11 auxiliary officers and 48 airmen. During the camp "officers have been given practice in carrying out reconnaissance, aerobatics, formation and general flying, whilst those not so far advanced are given instruction in flying on service types of aircraft. A series of inter-flight matches, tennis, cricket and football matches have also taken place."

AUXILIARY AIR FORCE CAMP

NORTH RIDING SQUADRON NEAR MIDDLESBROUGH

FROM OUR CORRESPONDENT

CATTERICK, AUG. 22

No. 608 (North Riding) Bomber Squadron, Auxiliary Air Force, to-morrow completes its annual training at Thornaby Aerodrome, near Middlesbrough, under the command of Squadron Leader W. Howard Davies. This aerodrome is not yet fully completed. Another shed is to be added to the existing one, a large institute is in the course of erection, and sleeping quarters are to be provided for officers. Thornaby Hall has been converted into an excellent officers' mess and the permanent staff are comfortably housed. This permanent staff consists of three officers (adjutant, assistant adjutant, and stores officer) and 33 rank and file all belonging to the Royal Air Force. The adjutant (Flight Lieutenant C. L. Falconer) is chief flying instructor. As in all newly-formed squadrons of under three years' existence, the assistant adjutant is also a flying instructor and assists in training.

The squadron went into camp on August 9 with 11 officers and 50 auxiliaries out of an establishment of 23 officers and 156 other ranks. The squadron will be completed to establishment as training facilities become available; recruiting is exceedingly good and there is keen competition to join. The standard of the recruits is very high. Nearly all the men come from the surrounding towns and villages and the officers from North Yorkshire. The squadron is equipped with four Wapiti and five Avro machines out of an establishment of 12 Wapiti and three Avros. Men who are learning to become fitters and metal riggers are allotted to machines and understudy and assist the regular *personnel* in all routine, inspections, and maintenance work.

On Wednesday the squadron was visited by Air Officer Commanding-in-Chief Air Defences Great Britain (Air Marshal Sir E. Ellington). The Air Officer Commanding No. 1 Defence Group (Group Captain Edmunds), to which the squadron belongs, also inspected the camp. The squadron gave an "at home" on middle Sunday, which was attended by 250 people, who were given tea and an exhibition of flying in which nine machines went up, led by the squadron leader.

The Times, Monday, Aug 24, 1931; pg. 12; Issue 45909; col D

An article in The Times on Monday 24th August 1931 spoke of the imminent end to 608 Squadron's summer camp and of the establishment of regular RAF personnel who were stationed at

Thornaby. "3 officers (adjutant, assistant adjutant and stores officer) and 33 rank and file. The adjutant, Flight Lieutenant C L Falconer is chief flying instructor." The article also notes that the squadron were visited by Air Officer Commanding-in-Chief Air Defences Great Britain, Air Marshal Sir E Ellington, and The Air Officer Commanding No 1 Defence Group, Group Captain Edmunds also inspected the camp."

It is apparent from the number of articles which grace the local press in the early days of the aerodrome that the public were very interested in what was going on there and on the impact that activities were having on day-to-day life in Thornaby. All local newspapers talk about both the aerodrome and 608 Squadron with pride and are enthusiastic about its presence in the area. Indeed, even discussion about expenditure on the aerodrome was reported in the local press. In 1932, the press reported on an RAF plane which crashed at Stockton. The Bristol Blenheim aircraft piloted by Flight Lieutenant Jones was being flown from Scotland to the South of England and was to call at Thornaby for refuelling. "The accident occurred shortly before eight o clock. Visibility at the time was very bad and the airman appeared to have lost his bearings for he circled round Stockton and Norton at a very low altitude three times before he attempted to land in the recreation ground. The machine crashed through a 6ft iron fence and turned a complete somersault before stopping. Neither the pilot nor any of the people on the ground were injured."

The local press were also keen to follow the lives of the young officers who were members of 608 Squadron, many of the young men had their marriages or engagements announced in the press with accompanying photographs.

The aerodrome was also part of the Air League of the British Empire's Empire Air Day programme where aerodrome's across the country were open to the public with a view to stimulate public interest in flying. The first open day was on Thursday May 24th 1934, and was widely reported in the local press. The aerodrome was open between 2pm and 8.30 pm and it was noted that "tea will be obtainable at a moderate charge from 4 to 8 pm. Buildings open to inspection will include the Drill Hall, Barrack Block and the Transport Section. Visitors will also be able to see in the workshops two air-cooled engines which will be stripped so that their mechanism may be understood. In the fabric room two uncovered air frames will be on view. Parties of visitors will be taken round the hangers under supervision. Flying training will be carried out in the air if the weather permits. This will include flight formations, camera obscura practice, and so on. Visitors will be admitted by the main entrance only." In 1934, the annual camp of the squadron took place and the establishment was noted as eleven officers and one hundred and eight other ranks. 608 Squadron was transferred to No 12 Group Fighter Command and was re-equipped with Hawker Demon aircraft. Squadron Leader G H Ambler assumed command. Geoffrey Ambler was the grandson of Sir James Hill, who was the owner of James Hill & Sons Ltd, the largest private wool merchants in the country, and also Liberal MP for Bradford Central. Geoffrey's father, Frederick Ambler, owned Midland Mills in Bradford, his mother, Annie Hill, was the sister of Sir James Hill. Geoffrey was born at Baildon in 1904 and was educated at Shrewsbury and rowed for the school at Henley in 1922. He attended Clare College, Cambridge where he obtained his BA degree and rowed in the winning university crews of 1924, 1925 and 1926. By 1930 he was Director of Fred Ambler Limited of Bradford, his father's woollen firm. A member of Yorkshire Aeroplane Club, he already had his pilot's license and owned his own plane.

Open day at Thornaby

Empire Air Day on Thursday May 24th 1934 meant that Thornaby Aerodrome was open to the public. The charge was one shilling per adult and sixpence for children. Visitors were able to view the aerodrome and its workings between 2 and 8pm, the idea being to stimulate public interest in flying and to strengthen links between the aerodrome and the local community. The local press reported that 3544 people visited Thornaby Aerodrome that day.

The first regular RAF personnel were assigned to Thornaby in 1935, No 9 Flying Training School who were equipped with Hawker Hart Trainer aircraft. The RAF Station Headquarters was not established until 1st June 1937 and Wing Commander J Leacroft MC was appointed as Station Commanding Officer with RAF Thornaby being assigned in No 16 Reconnaissance Group. The Operational record book notes that the policy was for there to be two general reconnaissance squadrons based at Thornaby and one AAF Fighter Squadron. In July 1937 RAF Thornaby became the base for No 224 and 233 (General Reconnaissance) Squadrons, each equipped with 18 Avro Anson aircraft. Between 15th November 1937 and 4th August 1939, RAF Thornaby was commanded by various officers including Group Captain A H Jackson, Wing Commander L G Le B Croke, Group Captain E O Grenfell and Group Captain S P Simpson. The Station remained in Coastal Command until 1st September 1938 when it was transferred to No 5 Group Bomber Command. During August and September 224 and 233 squadrons left Thornaby for Leuchars, being replaced by No's 106 and 105 Squadrons equipped with Fiery Battle aircraft. On 26th September 1938 106 and 185 Squadrons moved to war stations at Grantham, No 42 Squadron arrived and RAF Thornaby was ordered to take preparatory action to mobilization. On 28th September the role of the station was changed to 16 (Reconnaissance) Group, Coastal Command. Group. On 29th September 1938 269 Squadron arrived at Thornaby and on 7th October both 42 Squadron and 269 Squadron left. In the middle of October No's 106 and 185 Squadrons both returned. Captain Simpson had to announce the decision that 608 Squadron was to be re-designated as a General Reconnaissance Unit with 18 (Reconnaissance) Group. During the next two months the station was transferred from Bomber to Coastal Command and then back again. Then, early in 1939, RAF Thornaby was returned to No 18 Group Coastal Command. In August 1939 220 Squadron moved to Thornaby and began a four month conversion programme from

Avro Anson aircraft to Lockheed Hudson's.

The evidence studied, including the Operational Record Book, (ORB) of both 608 Squadron and RAF Thornaby Station, and the file on Thornaby Aerodrome located at Middlesbrough Archives suggests that an interesting relationship existed between the aerodrome and the local community. The initial building project required the employment of many skilled and unskilled men, and in many ways boosted the employment opportunities within the Teesside area. Also, by offering men the opportunity to volunteer to be part of the squadron, local industry and family businesses still continued to flourish. The relationship between the aerodrome and the local community was tense at times before the war. Between 1932 and 1936 Thornaby Council received a number of complaints from local residents who complained that their property valuations had been affected by low flying from the aerodrome. Comments were noted in January 1936, when a letter was sent from Thornaby Town Clerk to the Air Ministry stating that complaints regarding houses on land on west frontage of Thornaby Road and east frontage due to the Air Ministry decision to erect wooden huts. This has led to a reduction in the value of local houses. These complaints were echoed in the local press in February 1936.

Articles appeared in both the North Mail and the Newcastle Chronicle suggesting that the Aerodrome was flouting planning restrictions and regulations, and the erection of wooden huts, which were considered by some to be unsightly. A month later complaints were received again regarding noise from the machine gun range and engine testing apparatus. Added to this came a letter from the Town Clerk to the Thornaby Education Committee regarding complaints which have been received from Head Teachers of schools concerning intensive flying which is taking place over the town. It would appear that the local schools felt that there was open countryside to the South and West of the Aerodrome, which could be used for flying exercises rather than over the village of Thornaby itself.

Again in May, the Town Clerk was forced to write to the Air Ministry regarding complaints made by local residents suggesting that considerable machine gun firing was becoming intolerable. The Council asked the Air Ministry for removal of Butts to southern limits of Aerodrome to give the population of Thornaby some consideration. The Air Ministry responded on 6th June 1936 with the decision that a screening wall would be erected around the ranges, which would mitigate the noise. The Northern Echo again picked up these complaints on 10th June 1936. Finally, a petition was sent to Harold Macmillan, MP, from residents of dwelling houses at Thornaby asking for the removal of the machine gun firing butts. Noise and annoyance is intolerable. Babies scream, dogs howl and bark, horses bolt, spent bullets are found on Millbank Lane. Firing continues up to 8.30pm. Again the North East Daily Gazette picked this up on 22 July 1936, whose headline read Day sleepers disturbed.

These complaints highlight the problems that occurred during the 1930's with the growth of the Aerodrome, and the increase in flying that was taking place over Thornaby at weekends and on evenings. However, most of these issues had been ironed out by the time war was declared and as war approached it became clear to local residents that there was a great necessity for thorough training to take place to ensure that the region was prepared to defend itself during the ensuing hostilities and a much more positive relationship began to develop between the Aerodrome and the local community.

1935 saw establishment strength as 14 officers and one hundred and eight other ranks including new Pilot Officers S W Jackson, H J Williams, Peter Vaux, Harry Clayton and Geoffrey Whitley Garnett. The Times reported on May 26th 1936 of the appointment of Lord Swinton, Secretary of State for Air, as Honorary Air Commodore of No 608 (NR) Squadron. Then in August 1936, the officers and airmen of the squadron left Thornaby Aerodrome and headed to Tangmere to undergo a fortnight's annual training. The North Mail and Newcastle Chronicle noted that "in all probability it is the last occasion on which it will go into training as a bomber unit for on its return, it is to be converted into a defence squadron. At this year's camp the squadron is to carry out air firing drill with both front and back guns. It is also to be inspected by Sir John Steel, the Commander in Chief.

In 1937 the squadron was re-equipped with Demon two seat fighter aircraft and the squadron was transferred from a bomber squadron to a fighter squadron. The Northern Echo reported that 14 officers and 100 airmen paraded at Thornaby Aerodrome and were inspected by Air Commodore J C Quinnell, DFC, who stated "I find in this squadron a remarkable determination to succeed. An instance of this

is your band, your smart guard and your very high standard of drill.
Flying efficiency in the air depends on a good ground organisation
and you have succeeded in both respects." So on 5th May 1937 608
Squadron left the command of Air Commodore Quinnell and was
transferred to No 12 Fighter Group.

Sunday 18th July 1937 marked another Empire Air Day for 608
Squadron along with some one hundred Royal Air Force and civil air
stations. The idea behind the Empire Air Day was to show the two
sides of the country's air resources – military and civil – cooperating
to provide an opportunity for visitors at home and from overseas to
see British aviation from behind the scenes. This again strengthened
links between the local squadron and the community and removed
any suspicion or concern that local people may have had about the
function and make up of the aerodrome itself. This, it was hoped,
would improve relations between local residents, the local council
and the press. Lots of coverage was given in all the local press with
papers printing photographs and written reports on the day's
activities, thus raising awareness. The strength of the squadron on
that day was twelve officers and one hundred airmen. Visitors
included Lord Bolton, Lord-Lieutenant of the North Riding and his
wife, who inspected the men on parade.

During that year, other commissions as Pilot Officers were received
by J W Woolcock, P Johnson, C E J Dingle, D G Brown, P G Grey and
S P Phillips. The Squadron was also visited by Rt Honourable
Viscount Swinton GBE MC, Honorary Air Commodore of the
Squadron on 20th August 1937. The Squadron spent their annual
camp at Ramsgate and Major C C Turner, Air Correspondent from
the Daily Telegraph noted that "no auxiliary squadron represents a
greater diversity of occupations. Among those represented by the
officers here are the steel, textile, timber, coal, chemical, tanning and
printing industries. There are 130 of the squadron auxiliaries in
camp. There is a waiting list to join as airmen and no fewer than 80%
of the airmen are in private life process workers and fitters in ICI."

Later that year Air Commodore T L Leigh-Mallory under whose
command is the 12th Fighter Group, visited Thornaby Aerodrome to
present an official crest signed and approved by King George VI. The
Squadron was congratulated on its smartness and efficiency. "The
inscription on the crest could be interpreted as 'Tooth and Nail' or
always being ready if the necessity arose, to ascend into the air to

combat their enemies tooth and nail. A falcon's claw In a striking attitude is the design of the crest" noted the local press. Flight Lieutenant Keith Pyman of Far End, Yarm and Aircraftman Knott had a remarkable escape from death when their Demon Fighter crashed at High Worsall near the Richmond Road toll bar.

Whilst on the aerodrome, the men worked in normal jobs throughout the week, and then spent maybe two evenings a week and Saturdays and Sundays at the aerodrome. On weekday evenings they would arrive at the airfield just after work, say before six o'clock, and leave about nine thirty. The planes would be serviced and maintained and the officers and men would attend lectures. On weekends, they would arrive at nine in the morning and then stay till around teatime on the Sunday. They would have lectures, training, flying and night flying, as well as target practice. The early AAF insisted that volunteers for commission as a pilot had to be in possession of the civilian Pilot's "A" licence prior to his appointment. Flying instruction was then reinforced to the standard of a Royal Air Force Flying Training School on both dual and solo flights. The necessary tests and examinations were then undertaken before the award of the pilot's wings. Since training was generally given over weekends, this award of pilot's wings could take anything between eighteen months and two years.

The 10th July 1938 saw Thornaby Aerodrome holding another "At Home" with visitors including Lord and Lady Bolton, Air Commodore Leigh-Mallory, Air Commodore A J Godman, Deputy Lord Lieutenant of the North Riding, Air Commodore T E B Howe, Lieutenant Colonel and Mrs Chaytor, Major and Mrs Parrott and Group Captain H Grenfell. The Mayor and Mayoresses of Middlesbrough and Thornaby also attended. The Squadron gave an air display including individual acrobatics, squadron formation and dive past in salute.

At the end of September 1938 Squadron Leader Ambler left 608 Squadron to take over command of 609 (West Riding) Squadron. The Operational Record Book notes that on 2nd October 1938 a big dinner dance took place attended by two hundred and fifty officers and guests. A further officer's ball took place on Friday October 21st reported on widely by the local press. On 29th October 1938 there was also a guest night in honour of Squadron Leader Ambler. Flight Lieutenant Geoffrey Shaw was promoted to acting Squadron Leader and took over command of the squadron. Geoffrey Shaw came from Nunthorpe and his family owned W G Shaw Engineering Co in North Ormesby. His father, W G Shaw, was the President of the Middlesbrough branch of the Institute of British Foundry men. Geoffrey was educated in Scotland but then attended Cambridge University where he learned to fly as part of the University Air Squadron. The press reported in 1932 that "it is probably the distinction of Mr Geoffrey Shaw of Messrs W Shaw and Co Ltd, the Middlesbrough firm of steel founders to be the first owner of a private aeroplane in Middlesbrough, if not the whole of Cleveland. He intends to use the machine for long business trips." He took part in the MacRobertson Air Race from England to Australia in 1934 which was widely reported in the local press, who noted "a lone Middlesbrough flier, engaging on his first real long distance flight, and pitting his chances against all the energies of some of the wealthiest flying concerns in the world. That is the position of Flight Lieutenant Geoffrey Shaw who has entered his new plane in the England to Australia air race in October."

John Pollock's Collection

Other recruits to the squadron included John Newhouse, who came from one of the villages outside Middlesbrough, from the family that owned Newhouse's Department Store in Middlesbrough. William Appleby-Brown came from Saltburn; his father, James Brown, worked for the family firm J Brown and Co who were builder's merchants at Queens Square in Middlesbrough. The Brown family were prominent in Middlesbrough and included Alderman John Wesley Brown, who was MP for the town in 1921. William joined the family firm at a young age. His family also had a shipping company called Lion Shipping that imported iron ore from Spain and Timber from the Baltic States. They were very friendly with the Baird, Wrightson and Crosthwaite families. By the same token, the Appleby-Browns often visited the home of Sir Thomas Wrightson at Neasham and Eryholme. Dennis Baird came from West Hartlepool and his family business was importing various timber from the Baltic and Russia. Harry Clayton's family owned a well-known retail business in Middlesbrough and finally the families of Anthony Neville Wilson and C W Wright were clothiers in the Tower House in Middlesbrough.

Many officers in 608 had landed connections. For example, Peter Vaux was born in Grindon near Sunderland, went to school at Harrow, then went to Cambridge where he joined the University Air Squadron and learned to fly. He was commissioned into the Auxiliary Air Force in July 1933 and lived at Piercebridge in County Durham. He was the son of Colonel Ernest Vaux of Brettanby Manor, Barton. He was also an amateur jockey who rode in the Grand National, took part in various point-to-points, and rode with the Zetland and Bedale Hunts. At a lower level of landed society, George Williams, another pre-war pilot with 608 Squadron, born in Shrewton, near Salisbury in 1917, attended St Probus Prep School in Salisbury and then went on to boarding school in Cornwall, before studying at Cambridge University. His father was a gentleman farmer who was also a district and county councillor and Justice of the Peace. Similarly, Keith Pyman lived outside Yarm where his family were gentlemen farmers, and James Robertson from Saltburn also came from a farming family.

Other young recruits came from landed backgrounds but then worked for major companies or professions; for example, Philip Lloyd-Graeme, later Sir Philip Cunliffe Lister, was a member of the

Lloyd-Graeme family from Sewerby Hall and estate in the East Riding of Yorkshire. His father-in-law was Sir John Cunliffe-Lister, Baron of Masham and chief shareholder in Manningham Mills. Philip was educated at Winchester and University College Oxford. Later he was a barrister, Conservative MP and was three times President of the Board of Trade. John Sherburn Priestly (Pip) Phillips was born in Dublin in November 1919; his father John Skelton Phillips was in the army whilst his mother was related to J B Priestly. He attended St Olave's School in York before moving to the senior school, St Peter's School in York, on 23rd January 1933 where he was a full boarder. He left the school in July 1936 and moved to Crooksbarn Lane in Norton; Stockton on Tees. He was a successful rower for the school and a cadet in the OTC. He worked as an engineer in Darlington, employed by the London North Eastern Railway, joining 608 Squadron in 1937 at the age of 18. P Kennedy came from Middlesbrough and was an accountant at ICI and Ivo W H Thompson was the son of Sir Wilfrid and Lady Thompson of Old Nunthorpe.

At the beginning of 1939 J G Considing, R Bassett and J F Lambert were commissioned as Pilot Officers and by February of that year, the squadron strength was 19 officers and 185 other ranks with a total of 185 flying hours. On 20th March 1939 the squadron changed from a fighter to a general reconnaissance squadron flying Anson's. By May 1939 squadron strength stood at 21 officers and 267 other ranks. In June Pilot Officer Appleby-Brown was awarded the flying badge. By the time the squadron left for summer camp at Warmwell, squadron strength was 24 officers and 278 other ranks.

In 1939 608 Squadron attended their annual two-week summer camp at Warmwell, near Weymouth in Dorset but this was cut short by the impending war and the squadron received a signal giving one hour's notice to return to Thornaby at 1600 hours on 23rd August 1939. The Squadrons 24 officers and 278 other ranks, together with 18 Ansons, one Hart and two Tutors had to move fast to return to their home base. By 1810 the order had been given to return to Thornaby at once and 10 Anson aircraft took off between 1900 and 1930. At 2300 the main party left Warmwell by official train and arrived at Stockton at 1100 hrs. On 24th August orders were received for the squadron to be embodied into the Royal Air Force for full time duties and calling up notices were sent to all personnel. Full embodiment took place on 28th August 1939.

Officer Recruitment

The recruitment process for young men in the early 1930s would have been very much based on the family status of the young men around the area at the time. The Commanding Officer of 608 Squadron would have been aware of which influential families had young sons who might be available to join the squadron. The young man might receive a letter from the Commanding Officer or the Adjutant of the Squadron. Approaches to these families were then made over lunches and an enquiry as to the availability of the said young men was established. Thus in the main, recruitment for the post of pilots, and therefore officers, within 608 Squadron was undertaken largely by word of mouth. Connections clearly mattered. Mr P Alexander noted those were the days when your parents had to guarantee that they had at least £30 in their bank to pay your messing bills, otherwise you couldn't become an officer candidate. The young men often knew each other well because they had been to the same public school. This helped to build a 'family' atmosphere within a squadron.

In terms of the AAF hierarchy the officers were kept separate from the men. They were accommodated at the Officer's Mess in Thornaby Hall. Most of their social activities took place within the mess. The Sergeants had their own mess, as did the Corporals and other ranks. Officers did not go into any of the other messes unless they were officially invited. The young officers in the mess had a Bat Man who looked after about six of them. The higher up the ranks that they got, the more likely it was that they would have their own Bat Man, or would share one with another officer of a similar or equivalent rank. Friday nights would be 'dining in' nights where formal mess kit had to be worn and all the officers had to be presentable. After the formal dinner, generally the older officers would retire for a quiet drink and the younger element would engage in various games. The young officers were very high-spirited. They would take part in various

41

high jinks, walking on the ceiling, or high cock a lorum, a violent form of leapfrog, and another game where they were on 'piggy back' and fought each other with a rolled up newspaper. If the young officers ventured out of the mess they tended to socialise in Yarm. The research notes that the young men were not much interested in Thornaby, and is supported by the fact that these young officers all had motorcars, which was unusual in the 1930s.

Mrs Appleby-Brown discussed what she perceived as the public-school atmosphere that existed within the mess, the connection between family businesses and industry and the home and family backgrounds of officers. For example, "the mess was very well controlled; it was controlled rather like a public school. It was their home background that enabled them to be officers, most of them were in family businesses you see, and family businesses weren't famous for paying big salaries. But you got time off, this was the great thing. ICI and some of the big firms wanted to assist the community, so again you could get time off. People volunteered to do things and this was considered to be good. You see if you had been at a boy's boarding school or a public school there were things that you had to do, you just got on with it. They were high-spirited, the younger element, very high spirited, but at the same time they turned out to be very reliable pilots."

She was convinced of the importance of public school training in shaping character and behaviour, "many of the young officers in 608 squadron had been to public school and public school taught them moral values, initiative, living as a community and public spirit. They were used to wearing school uniform and having to be properly dressed because that was the way of life for public school children in the 1920's and 1930's. All of these values and ideals and discipline were transferred from public school to the Officer's Mess.

Mr Coppick, a veteran who served with 608 Squadron prior to World War II noted that in those days there was a big separation between the officers and the men. In terms of the relationship between the regulars and the auxiliaries, he pointed out the auxiliaries had full time jobs and they were there at weekends. You had to ask people what they were. In fact the regulars were treated as outsiders. The auxiliaries all knew each other. Another veteran, Mr Sydney Buckle, who joined 608 Squadron in 1932 as a bomb aimer and air gunner stated that the officers and the airmen were separate because they had their own clubs and so forth. Another interviewee, Mr Albert Guy, who joined 608 Squadron in 1938 as a fitter aero engine felt that initially there was a problem with the relationships between the regulars and the auxiliaries. "We were always the weekend airmen you know. In every sense." That changed of course as the war advanced and more and more people kept coming into it. That diluted the squadrons. There was a lot of friction between the regular airmen and our members. If we met outside socially, comments were made and this sort of behaviour, "weekend fliers" and all that sort of rubbish. He also had very definite views about the relationship between the officers and the airmen within the squadron. "The auxiliary officers were all what we would call "the gentleman type", hare and hounds and field sports type. Amateur jockeys and that sort of thing. I found in my experience, bitterly that they did not really come round to the fact that we were on the same level so to speak. There was an officer class and an airman class and there was a gulf. It was more pronounced there than anywhere else I went in the service." He reinforces this view when he notes, you respect them of course. You only spoke when you were spoken to and you answered questions rather than asked them. You hardly ever saw them really. They were there and we were there and we had a job to do and we got on with it, and we never met them socially at all.

Ronnie Waterson, a Flight Mechanic who joined 608 Squadron in 1938 stated, the officers were the pilots and you had direct contact with them. You helped them get in, looked after the planes, filled them up and then helped them out. There was a divide between them. We had very little contact with the officers. Socially the officers did not go where we did. Even on summer camp I never mixed with the officers at all. Walter Davies, who joined 608 Squadron in 1933 and worked on the fabric section servicing planes had also spoken of a distinct gap between the officers and the airmen.

Finally, George Williams, one of the early pilots with 608 Squadron noted, class was a big factor pre-war. During the war those sorts of things tended to go out of the window. In the AAF all the pilots were commissioned, the NCOs were not. There was a definite divide between the two. We lived in different messes. The officers had different food, probably better food. Officers had batmen. Class was not an issue during the war. Time was too short. It was much more important in an Auxiliary squadron. I socialised with junior officers.

Usually the officers sat together and did not frequent the places where the airmen went.

Clearly a hierarchy existed within the AAF between the officers and the airmen. Each needed the other and each respected each other but there was little contact between the two in terms of social activities. However, it is apparent that this division had its advantages and was a crucial part of the AAF as a military organisation. It allowed for the AAF to maintain its image as a "gentleman's flying club" which gave it a certain aura of social exclusivity. This enabled it to attract the "right sort" throughout the 1930s.

The backgrounds of the original officers who were recruited to join 608 Squadron, and the interviews that have been conducted with men who served in the Squadron prior to the Second World War provide evidence to show that 608 Squadron was very much a class driven institution, and that this reflects the situation within all Auxiliary Air Force Squadrons in England, with recruitment based on background and status, rather than ability. There was a huge divide between the officers and the airmen and this is reinforced by their social activities and their work related activities. The relationships between the two were very much that of the officers being in charge and the men working for them to fulfil their needs and maintain their safety. The relationship was courteous within the hangers and on the runways, but once the work of the day was over, contact between the two groups rarely happened. This was due to a number of factors such as the possession of cars by the young officers which enabled them to travel further a field for their entertainment, and also because of the mess buildings which kept each rank separate from the others, unless by invitation. Only three of the pre-war officers had their own planes and in the main they came from family businesses within the Teesside locality. The airmen on the other hand could be trained for the trade that they wanted to learn, but flying was kept strictly for the officers.

Recruiting the Other Ranks

Mr J M Alexander's Collection

As early as 1930 adverts and reports were placed in the local newspapers to recruit men to fill the various positions available within both 608 Squadron and the Aerodrome. Craftsmen would be trained for their various jobs after they had joined the Squadron, which virtually meant the establishment of a new "industry" for the district. If a man was successful in securing a position as a craftsman on the aerodrome, he might not be called upon to follow his own particular craft. There was a strong probability that he would be trained in another branch by the specialist RAF instructors who would be stationed with the Squadron for that purpose. The recruiting age was 18-26. It is interesting to note that one year later, the same newspaper talks of the airmen enlisted as Aircraftmen 2nd Class, undergoing training in whichever trade they wished to take up. The early part of their training consisted of getting a thorough working knowledge of the basic principles of their trade; later they were taken by easy stages up to a point where they were examined by a trade test board and passed as having a good standard of knowledge in their particular trade. A candidate wishing to join as an auxiliary airman had the choice of several trades. He had however to be thoroughly fit and pass a medical examination before being accepted. His term of service would be for four years.

Looking at the press cuttings for the period up to 1946 there is no mention of the airmen other than to refer to the jobs that they did on the aerodrome. Specifically there is no mention of airmen by name, whereas on the other hand, the officers of the Squadron are covered regularly in terms of their out of Squadron activities, such as engagements, marriages or other successes. Interviews that have been conducted with veterans who served as airmen and NCOs within the Squadron will be used to show the difference in backgrounds that they had.

Harry Thrower was brought up in a mining village at Houghton and his father was a Methodist preacher. He left school at fourteen and worked as a miner. He decided to join 608 Squadron because he did not enjoy mining and thought that he could learn other skills within the Auxiliary Air Force. He met his wife through one of the dances that were held each week at the aerodrome. He worked as ground crew and he was responsible for the upkeep of Geoffrey Amblers plane. He was sent away on lots of courses to further his mechanical knowledge. His friends included a postman living at Thornaby and a chap who worked at ICI. He stated the regulars and the auxiliaries did not get on well together, but the regulars were there to train them in the servicing of aircraft, so they had to put up with it.

Harold Coppick was born in Manor Street in Middlesbrough and joined the AAF in 1936. His reason for joining was because he was working for ICI he knew that war was coming on because they said if anybody joined the forces they would get their wages made up in spite of what they were earning in civvy street. Socially he would go to the Odd Fellows public house, or to the Squadron dances, but he was very clear that the officers and the airmen did not mix socially.

Bob Harbron had been aware of the aerodromes presence since he was a young boy when he would go and watch the planes taking off and landing. He was born in Billingham and went to school in Norton near Stockton on Tees. In civilian life he was employed by Head Wrightsons as an apprentice engineer. He joined 608 Squadron and spoke of the gulf between the officers and the airmen, which existed.

> "You saluted the officers, you spoke when you were spoken too; you answered their questions about their plane. That was it, other than that you were never in contact with them."

Syd Buckle was born in Thornaby and his father was a builder. He left school at fourteen and worked for a sign painter for a while. He joined 608 in 1932 as an air gunner and bomb aimer. He pointed out

> "all the local pilots were officers of course, no one else was allowed to fly before the war. The officers I came into contact with were okay, you see there were officers who were not flying, of the officers I came into contact with, there would be about a dozen officers who were actual fliers."

Albert Guy joined 608 Squadron prior to the war. He was born in Barnard Castle. His father had been a member of the Royal Flying Corps in World War I. His father was a corporal whose job it was to chauffer one of the top commanders of the Royal Flying Corps in France. When the RFC became the Royal Air Force in 1918, his father served for a further two years. On leaving the RAF, his father worked for the United Bus Company because he had been a driver in the RFC. He then set up a taxi business in Newton Aycliffe, County Durham. He joined 608 Squadron because he was aware that there was going to be a war. At the time, he was working for the United Bus Company. He enlisted when he was seventeen years and ten months old, the minimum age for new volunteers. His selected trade was FAE, Fitter Aero Engines and he received full training whilst at Thornaby. He served at Thornaby for two years and pointed out that it was busy as a station goes.

> "It didn't do a great deal, not 608 Squadron anyway. 220 Squadron was the regular air force unit that was there, flying

Hudson's. They did a lot of work, but we were always in the background somehow, 608 Squadron. We had the Anson's and they were out there doing what we called the Kipper Patrol, flying convoys up the North East Coast."

He pointed out that there was a great team spirit among the airmen because they were all doing the same job. Two of his friends joined 608 Squadron when he did, and they both worked for the United Bus Company before the War. He noted,

"it was a marvellous experience, I never regretted at all joining it. I had no regrets about that. I enjoyed the social life; the Maison was the best dance hall in Stockton. I enjoyed the attention from the girls, one of the best things was that I would be paid expenses to get to Thornaby, so much a mile you know, and the very fact that I worked at the United Bus Company gave me a free pass on the buses, so it cost me nothing at all to get to Thornaby, and I got paid that every three to four months. They paid me for my service there as well. I got fourteen shillings a fortnight less barrack damages. That was a lot more than I got as an apprentice. I used to get six shillings and eight pence a week in those days, and I used to give half of it to my mother for my keep. So what I got there was all mine. Plus my travelling money back. So I was better off as an auxiliary airman travelling backwards and forwards to Thornaby that I was as a civilian."

On leaving the AAF after World War II he joined a small factory called Crowbrough Engineering Company, as a toolmaker.

Ronnie Waterson was born on 15th December 1917 in Sunderland. His family moved to Billingham when he was a child. His father was an electrician at ICI, and his mother was a shop assistant at the Coop. He left school at age fourteen and worked as an errand boy at a grocers shop before moving to ICI in the fertilizer-packing department. He joined 608 Squadron in 1938 because he was aware that there was likely to be a war and he would be called up. He wanted to join the service that he was interested in. He trained to be a flight mechanic and served with the Squadron up until 1942. He stated

"we had very little contact with the officers before the war started because we were going on training. We used to fill up with petrol, check the tyres and so on. On a night we would go to the Odd

Fellows and we would sit with our friends. I only went on one summer camp, that was at Warmwell and I never mixed with the officers at all. The ranks were kept separate by the buildings and the uniform."

He also pointed out that

"some of the officers worked at ICI, very few like. We had Sergeants and Corporals that worked at ICI that I knew from the Squadron. When asked about ICI's reaction to the AAF he stated Well I don't think they minded. I worked at ICI. I think they encouraged it if I am not mistaken."

Walter Davies was born in Redcar in 1915. His father worked for a shipping agent in Middlesbrough. His mother didn't work at all. He left school at fourteen and started work on a milk round with a milkman. He then worked for an engineering firm in Middlesbrough. He joined 608 Squadron in 1933 when he was eighteen years old. He worked on the fabric section of the aeroplane, not the engineering. He left 608 Squadron in 1945 as a Sergeant. After the war he came home and took over his father in laws business, which was a tobacconist. He did that for a while and then went to Risdales Analytical Chemists where he stayed until he retired.

A Selection of Veterans Photographs

Mr Harold Coppick's Collection

Mr J M Alexander's Collection

Mr Harold Coppick's Collection

Mr A Guy's Collection

Mr J M Alexander's Collection

Mr J M Alexander's Collection

Mr C W Gilbert's Collection

Mr C W Gilbert's Collection

Mr C W Gilbert's Collection

Mr C W Gilbert's Collection

Mr J M Alexander's Collection

Mr C W Gilbert's Collection

Mr G Davies's Collection

Mr G Davies's Collection

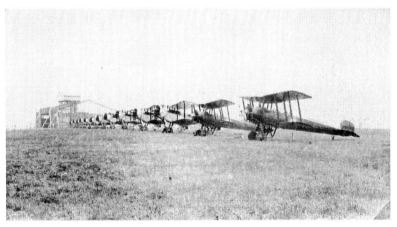

Mr J M Alexander's Collection

Mr J M Alexander's Collection

Mr J M Alexander's Collection

Mr John Pollock's Collection

Mr John Pollock's Collection

Mr John Pollock's Collection

Mr John Pollock's Collection

Mr John Pollock's Collection

Mr John Pollock's Collection

The War Years at the Aerodrome

War broke out on September 3rd 1939 and one of the first duties of the preparation for war was the air inspection of the camouflage of ICI and other industrial plants in the area. Colour aerial photographs were taken for the first time. The airfield also had to be camouflaged, its buildings were covered with tar and wood chippings and pre-camouflaged wire mesh was used to disguise awkward shapes. Gas blankets were used to black out windows, walls were built to protect the refuelling tankers and huts and the old radio station was taken down and a new 6000kc's frequency was installed which had a direct contact to Teesside Gunnery Control at Elton Hall. Large numbers of barrack blocks were erected to cope with the influx of new staff. On the 13th September 1939 Anson aircraft from 220 Squadron sighted and attacked a U Boat on the surface of the North Sea but it escaped without damage. On the 8th November 1939 Hudson N7290 from 220 Squadron stalled on approach to the Aerodrome and crashed into a house in Cambridge Road Middlesbrough. All the crew were killed. 1st November 1939 saw a visit to the Aerodrome by King George VI.

On 1st December 1939 the first detachment of Women's Auxiliary Air Force personnel reported to the accounts officer for duty. A further accident for 220 Squadron occurred ten days later on the 18th November when Hudson N2784 crashed into the sea five miles east of Seaham. Throughout 1940 220 Squadron suffered several other accidents, all of which can be found in the appendices. In February 1930 a "Moonbeams Concert Party" took place on the station.

In July 1941, No 6 Operational Training Unit (OTU) arrived at Thornaby with the job of training general reconnaissance crews. 23rd March 1943 saw the arrival of No 1 OTU whose job was the training of pilots, air-observers and wireless operator/air-gunners. They remained at Thornaby until they were disbanded on 19th October 1943.

Mr J M Alexander's Collection

On 12th December all footpaths, bridle paths etc in the airfield area were closed to the public and marked with notices reading "Police Notice. This right of way is temporarily closed. By Order." Personnel from the Women's Auxiliary Air Force began to arrive at Thornaby during 1940, taking up positions in the Motor Transport Section, Photographic Section, Wireless and Radar Sections and in the Operations Room. On the night of the 4th June 1940 Thornaby aerodrome was bombed and two Hudson's, serial numbers N7309 and P5157 were destroyed whilst being refuelled and two bowsers (fuel tankers) were destroyed. Six bombs were dropped alongside the runway. On 8th June 1940 two more unexploded bombs were found on the airfield. On average, two air raids a day occurred. Several pillboxes, which were low concrete gun emplacements were placed around the airfield to ensure it was adequately defended; five pillboxes, each crewed by four men, were sited along the east side of Stainsby Beck. Another was sited next to Thornaby Woods and four more were located at the top of Leven Bank to protect the runways.

In February 1940, Hudson aircraft from 220 Squadron located the Altmark, a supply ship for the German pocket battleship Graf von Spee, in Josing Fjord. It was believed that the ship was returning to Germany with British prisoners on board. On 16th February, the destroyer HMS Cossack boarded the Altmark and freed the prisoners.

In June German aircraft bombed the airfield while planes were practising. One airman was killed. This prompted the decision by Thornaby Town Council to evacuate everyone living within 1000 yards of the airfield. This decision was never carried out. In December barbed wire was strung out along Millbank Lane. Since the war had begun, 350 air raid warnings had sounded in Thornaby.

In November 1940 the first civilian QL (lighting) and QF (fire) decoy night sites began to appear across Teesside. The idea had come from Colonel J F Turner who worked for the Ministry of Defence and from January 1940 began to lay out dummy aerodromes. Q sites were built to ensure that the Germans had to fly over them before reaching their main target. QL sites had a series of strategically placed lights to simulate buildings and industry. They had machines that were designed to give out orange sparks to give the appearance of trams moving, furnaces and so on. QF sites had controlled fires set to simulate factories, stores, ammunition dumps and so on. The idea being that they would look as if a bomb had been dropped and exploded in that area so that enemy planes would leave the site and go elsewhere to drop their bombs. Between June and December 1940 227 attacks were made on these decoy sites.

There was also a decoy airfield that was manned by twenty airmen and was located near Grange town, Middlesbrough between Lazenby Village and the trunk road. It was called a K site and had full size dummy Blenheim aircraft, which cost £150 each, and Vauxhall even produced an inflatable model of the Bedford truck. It had a control tower, gun placements and a variety of airfield buildings. A QL site was added to this, which consisted of a flare path and circuit lights that were set up to represent the runways at Thornaby. There was also another dummy airfield, which was operated by two men at Middleton-St-George, this was known as Goosepool. The idea was that the lights would be turned off just as the German pilot saw them. The pilot would then think that a blackout had occurred and would come off his flight path and bomb the dummy airfield.

In March 1941 114 (Hong Kong) Squadron was transferred into No 18 Group Coastal Command to perform coastal patrols and anti-shipping strikes flying Blenheim's. It moved to Leuchars in May 1941. On July 19th No 6 Operational Training Unit (OTU) arrived at Thornaby to train crews on Hudson aircraft. They also used Greatham satellite airfield at West Hartlepool for circuit and bump training (take off and landing). Also in July 143 Squadron arrived from Aldergrove and remained at Thornaby until September of that year, flying Beaufighter F Mk 1c aircraft. In September barbed wire was strung round the whole of the airfield perimeter to act as defence against intruders. On 10th December 1941 RAF Thornaby came under the command of Wing Commander C D Candy. Eight days later, a Lockheed Hudson, reputedly of 608 Squadron crashed into farm at Ingleby Barwick; eleven people were killed including the crew of seven. In February of 1942 Group Captain E D H Davies became Commanding Officer of RAF Thornaby. In June, Hudson's of 6 OTU took part in a raid on Bremen. One aircraft failed to return. On 13th July Group Captain M R Kelly OBE took over as Commanding Officer of RAF Thornaby. For the third Thousand-Bomber raid that took place on the night of 25/26 June 1942 twelve Hudson's from 6 OTU took part in the raid together with twelve from the other Hudson OTU at Silloth who were deployed to Thornaby for the raid. There were two Czechoslovakian Flights that were part of 6 OTU and their job was to provide crews for the two Wellington Squadrons in Coastal Command.

In January 1942 two concerts were put on in the Station Drill Hall, "The Spotlights" and "Aladdin" which were enjoyed by many of the personnel on the Aerodrome. In March 1943 6 OTU were replaced at Thornaby by 1 OTU who were flying Hudson aircraft and remained at Thornaby until they disbanded in October 1943. Part of 1 OTU was Czechoslovakian 1429 Flight whose job was to train Hudson crews. They remained at Thornaby until 1 OTU disbanded on 19th October 1943. On 11th and 12th March two bombs were dropped on the town of Thornaby. One fell on the Britannia Hotel and also demolished four houses. The other dropped on the electric power station on Mandale Road at 11.30pm, also damaged was the Church of England School. In all, one person was killed. During this time, Thornaby had been covered by two fighter detachments from Catterick for patrol dutics. From the beginning of January until January 20th one section of 403 Squadron Royal Canadian Air Force were based at Thornaby flying Spitfire Vb's, they were replaced by 401 Squadron RCAF and remained at Thornaby flying Spitfire Vb's until they were replaced on 29th May by 306 (Polish) Squadron also flying Spitfire Vb's. The Polish squadron left Thornaby on 11th August 1943 to move to Gravesend.

On 28th August Group Captain B Paddon DSO took over as Commanding Officer of RAF Thornaby. Thornaby had become part of 16 Group Coastal Command and had become engaged in air sea rescue. In October 1943 the ASR Training Unit arrived equipped with Vickers Warwick aircraft. It was joined by 280 Squadron equipped with Anson's, they were immediately reequipped with Warwick's. On November 21st the Warwick Training Unit arrived from Bircham Newton and on 22nd November 281 Squadron reformed with an establishment of Warwick's as an ASR unit. In December the Air Sea Rescue Training Unit moved to Thorney Island, and in February 1944 281 Squadron moved to Tiree. They were replaced by the Air Sea Rescue Training Unit.

In May 1944 the Air Sea Rescue Training Unit moved to Turnbury and 280 Squadron moved to Strubby. In June the Warwick Training Unit also left leaving the status of Thornaby from June 6th 1944 as a detachment of 280 Squadron as part of No 16 Group. In October 1944 279 Squadron arrived from Bircham Newton with Hudson's and soon converted to Warwick's. They remained at Thornaby until September 3rd 1945. Also, during this time, aircraft and crews including ground staff of 455 Squadron Royal Australian Air Force moved to Thornaby. They left during May 1945.

At the beginning of 1945 a small number of Hawker Hurricanes were added to the establishment of 279 Squadron. Following the end of the war, on 7th October Group Captain J M D Ker assumed command of RAF Thornaby and on 23rd October Thornaby Road was re-opened.

War-time Duties for 608 Squadron

608 Squadron were mobilized on 1st September 1939, although pilot training lectures continued. By the end of the month the squadron strength stood at 25 officers and 379 other ranks flying convoy patrols and Anti-submarine patrols. The first operational flight took place on 21st September 1939 when Squadron Leader Geoffrey Shaw, Flying Officer Woolcock, L A C Kelly and Corporal Knott took off on an anti-submarine patrol in Anson N5207. This flight proved to be a false alarm. From October 5th 608 Squadron, equipped with Avro Ansons, became operational in convoy escort role. On 6th October Pilot Officer J Scott was accidentally killed in a motorcycle accident. Whilst on 27th October 1939 Anson N5204 UL-N was on routine patrol when it was shot down near the Humber Lightship by a Hurricane from RAF Digby. Pilot Officer A Baird, Flight Lieutenant G Garnett and Cpl Wilson were all killed and HMS Stork was able to recover the body of Aircraftsman Smith. On 2nd February 1940 Anson N199 UL-M was forced to land in the sea following engine failure. The aircraft sank after 45 minutes and a minesweeper 6 miles off Blyth was able to pick up the crew of Flying Officer Johnson, Pilot Officer Lambert, AC2 Lumley and Corporal Young.

On 16th June 1940 Anson N5067 UL L hit high-tension cables in bad visibility and crashed near Brotton. Pilot Officer Duncan was injured and Sergeant L Walpole died of his wounds three days later. In December 1939 608 Squadron took delivery of its new Blackburn Botha aircraft and they were used by the squadron between June and November 1940 alongside the Anson's. They were the only squadron to use the aircraft operationally using it for coastal patrols carrying 100 lb anti-submarine bombs. The Botha was severely underpowered and unstable and there were a number of fatal crashes in 1940 which resulted in the Air Ministry withdrawing the aircraft from operations and transferring them to training units instead. Thus on August 24th Botha L6209 UL-O set off on a convoy escort mission but the engine out out after take off and the Botha was belly landed hitting a ditch at Ormesby. The crew on this occasion were Pilot Officer D Horner and Pilot Officer Reid. On 31st August 1940 Botha L6165 UL took off on a training flight but was unable to land. The aircraft was presumed to have ditched in the North Sea with the crew of Pilot Officer Creed, Pilot Officer Barrett, AC1 T Corrigan and AC2 G Beadnall.

In 1940 608 Squadron were flying Blackburn Botha's, but a change of aircraft took place in April 1941, 608 Squadron were fully operational on Blenheim 4's and did many long-range patrols along Danish coast. On 30 June 1941 Blenheim IV Z5982 UL-L ditched while searching for a dingy killing its crew Pilot Officer Sir I MacRobert, Sgt A Best, Sgt H Hillwood and Flying Officer R Keating. On 7th September Hudson V AM601 UL-N crewed by Sgt Harrington, Sgt Foster, Sgt Bennett and Sgt T Corrie took off to provide air cover for convoy EC70. The Hudson overshot the runway at 2245 hours during a night landing at Thornaby and crashed into valley beyond the runway. The first operational flight was on the 21st September - an anti-submarine patrol, which was a response to a false alarm. The number of operational sorties increased month by month so that by April 1940 the monthly total was 131. Duties included convoy escorts, anti-submarine patrols, air-sea rescue missions and coastal patrols searching for sight of possible German invasion forces. On 20th October Hudson V AM523 UL-F took off with two other squadron aircraft. After failing to find any shipping the flight turned to attack the Thisted seaplane base. The Hudson dropped its bombs on the slipway and was then seen to make a vertical bank. It was not seen again until aircraft crews saw it burning. The crew at this time were Sgt A Hendy, Sgt S Symons, Sgt W Wright and Sgt W White.

On 27th October the squadron suffered its first operational casualties when Anson N5204 was shot down into the North Sea by a Hurricane from Digby. As a result orders were received to repaint the roundels of red, white and blue and for all aircraft on convoy escort duties to leave their undercarriages down. It would appear however that the local recruitment and training of officers and airmen paid off because the local knowledge of the squadron enabled them to defend their area efficiently. Also in this month 220 Squadron left RAF Thornaby for Wick.

Mr J M Alexander's Collection

The Times of 21st February 1941 noted the award of a Distinguished Flying Cross for Wing Commander Geoffrey Shaw, whilst local press reported on 28th March 1941 that "Teesside 'week-end' fliers are marking war history." It talks of how "generally speaking, the war record of this squadron will be a tale of hard slogging on general reconnaissance work in good weather and foul, at all times of the year, of nerve wracking hours spent at tugging controls while shepherding convoys along the North-East coast, or patrolling enemy coastlines, ever conscious of the German fighters waiting to pounce." In May Squadron Leader Shaw left 608 Squadron after three years in command and a total of eleven years with the Squadron. Wing Commander RS Darbyshire took over as CO.

The 22nd July 1941 saw reports of the death of Squadron Leader Patrick Stuart Hutchinson who was killed on active service. 608 Squadron then started flying training on Hudson aircraft. Also during this month 6 Operational Training Unit arrived at Thornaby to train crews on Anson and Hudson aircraft. In October 608 Squadron attacked ports and airfields of Aalborg and other targets in Norway and Denmark. They also made several leaflet drops, raids and strikes off Dutch Coast. Wing Commander RS Darbyshire was killed during a shipping strike with 608 Squadron on 5th November 1941 when his Hudson, V AM 657 UL-D failed to return from its mission. Other crew members included Pilot Officer J Berry, Sgt S Mandall and Flying Officer G Hoar. Squadron Leader D P R Hutchings took over command. Squadron Leader Hutchings was to win the DFC with 608 Squadron and become a Wing Commander.

On 16th November 1941 Hudson V AM883 UL-N flew into high ground 2 miles west of Lumsden killing Flight Sergeant R Wood, Sgt R Neville, Sgt L Pain, whilst Sgt Shuidan was injured. On 23rd November Hudson V AM715 UL-T on a routine patrol over Norway suddenly plunged down and struck a fence. One of the crew was thrown clear but died as a result of wounds received. The crew members killed were Flight Sergeant George Fullerton, Flight Sergeant Russell Macmillan, both of the Royal Canadian Air Force, and Sgt John Short and Francis Simmonds. At the end of December 608 (NR) Squadron left RAF Thornaby after eleven years and moved to Wick, before moving overseas to take part in the Allied invasion of North Africa.

What becomes apparent following the Squadrons embodiment into the RAF is that the number of regular personnel who were transferred from other squadrons into 608. This clearly diluted the squadron in terms of fewer and fewer auxiliary volunteers remaining in the squadron, so that by March 1942, Australian, Canadian, Polish and American aircrew, as well as aircrew from all parts of the British Isles, combined with the few auxiliaries still flying. Indeed, an article in the Gazette on 28th March 1941 stated "up to the outbreak of the war, the 608th Squadron consisted entirely of local personnel...the outbreak of war found this unit away from its aerodrome...pilots were quickly sent away to become operationally trained and regular flying personnel was drafted in to fill the temporary deficiency. All the pilots sent away for additional training did not come back to their original unit. Many were finally drafted into fighter and bomber squadrons in other parts of the country...few of the original members of the 608th Squadron now remain with the unit. Two new pilots, JCT Downey and T C Stansbury, both serving in the RAF on regular commissions, joined the squadron."

The other interesting point is that as the war began to develop, from 1940 onwards, sergeants, such as Sergeant Burton and Sergeants Gowing and Norton, were being used to fly planes. This had not happened previously and demonstrates the need for more men capable of flying aircraft. Clearly as the war progressed, there were less and less officers available to fly because of the number of men being killed, injured or posted to other squadrons and the gap that was left had to be filled by men from the other ranks. The other important point is that as the planes used by Coastal Command became bigger, they needed more men to crew them, and clearly there were not enough officers to be able to do that.

George Crow was a member of the regular Royal Air Force but served at Thornaby during the war remembered that

"608 Squadron were active doing submarine patrols and air sea rescue and that sort of thing, and I remember the aircraft 608 had at that particular time, they were what the Americans had sent us on Lease-Lend, Lockheed Hudson's."

He noted

"we shared the mess and everything with 608 people. We, myself and the other technicians were actually out on the dispersal of the Aerodrome. The closeness with flying types and ground types was very close because you were signing your name to say that the aircraft was serviceable to fly, and you worked together and you messed together and you became quite a little unit. We knew the men in 608, we messed together. I can tell you a funny story. At mess time, if it was fish, we used to say "oh fish for dinner, 608 has been out on ops. They would throw things at us. There was that sort of bantering going on."

He said that the relationship between the officers and the airmen was good

"I have loaned money to a lot of the officers. They had to buy their own uniforms and they had a mess bill and they didn't have

71

the money that we had. All I could see about PO's and Flying Officers was that they did not have much money. Sometimes they had to turn up at mess do's and buy drinks when they couldn't afford it. Some, when they got their mess bill were a "bit pushed for the ready" and would perhaps borrow a fiver to tide them over till payday. I have had fish and chips out of Pilot Officers hats when we had been on a boozy trip."

This would suggest that during the war there was a more relaxed relationship between the officers and the airmen.

From September 1940 onwards much of the old spirit that had belonged to 608 Squadron was declining as its personnel were posted out to different squadrons and replacement intakes were coming in from other squadrons. The Gazette in 1941 talked of

"Teesside weekend fliers making war history" and though it retold stories of original members of 608 squadron who had been posted to fighter and bomber command, "generally speaking, the war record of this squadron will be a tale of hard slogging on general reconnaissance work in good weather and foul, at all times off the year, of nerve-wracking hours spent at tugging controls while shepherding convoys along the North East coast, or patrolling enemy coastlines ever conscious of the German fighters waiting to pounce."

The writer went on to highlight how important a place that the squadron held in local people's minds stating

"it will be gratifying to the people of Teesside as it was encouraging to the members of the squadron that all the vital work had not escaped the eyes of the Air Ministry, and the unit has four times been mentioned in despatches and there had been two Distinguished Flying Crosses awarded. Few of the original members of the 608 Squadron now remained with the unit. There has been the inevitable toll of warfare, and many are playing a heroic part with other squadrons. But the tradition of the unit still remains, and when the exploits of each section are fully revealed, they will make an outstanding contribution towards the great part Teesside is playing in winning the war."

Technological advances in aircraft design and production also resulted in large bombers requiring increasingly large crews. 608

Squadron was equipped in July 1941 with the Lockheed Hudson, which required a crew of six. As crew size increased, some of the rear gunners and navigators became airmen. A co-pilot was also needed because the aircraft had a much longer range for flying. In the first instance, a second officer filled the co-pilots role, but as the war progressed, a shortage of officers led to more NCO pilots being used, first as co-pilots then as pilots themselves. These technological advancements – increases in maximum speeds and range, amounts of weaponry and crew – reinforce the view that the AAF officers within 608 Squadron could not supply the necessary manpower for these planes on a regular basis, and this transformed the structure and culture of the squadron.

During 1941 the Squadron was re-equipped with Bristol Blenheim's and then Hudson aeroplanes with airborne radar leading to a more offensive role including, dropping leaflets over Denmark, and bombing enemy airfields. On the 18th December 1941 a Hudson from 608 Squadron crashed into a farm at Ingleby Barwick killing the crew of seven and a further 4 people. "A ball of fire seemed to fall out of the sky over Eaglescliffe watched by the newly arrived number 5 intake of no.6 Coastal Command Operational Training Unit on 18th December 1941 when the worst accident at Thornaby occurred. HudsonV9032 of the training unit stalled on take off and crashed into Quarry Farm at Ingelby Barwick, 5 miles from the aerodrome.

On 2nd January 1942 608 Squadron moved to Wick in the North of Scotland where they continued coastal reconnaissance, hunted for German U-boats and attacked the German cruiser Prince Eugen. On 5th August 1942 the squadron left Wick and moved to Sumburgh, and then on 25th August the main air party left for Gosport, arriving by 27th August. On 1st November 1942 the squadron boarded H M S Strathmore with 8 officers and 400 other ranks and left Gourock for an unknown destination. It was later revealed that the squadron was to take part in the occupation by American and British forces of French North Africa. HMS Strathmore was bound for the Port of Algiers.

On 5th November the squadron aircraft and all aircrews left North Coates for RAF Station Exeter. Then on the 9th November Squadron aircraft composed of 23 Mark V Hudson aircraft camouflaged white, left Exeter carrying all the squadron aircrew to Gibraltar. On 13th November the squadron ground personnel disembarked from HMS

Strathmore and marched to the Jardin D'Essai, Algiers where they spent the night. The next day they marched to the railway station and headed for Blida. On 16th December under orders from Eastern Air Command, some of the squadron flying personnel and those of the ground staff detached at Gibraltar flew to Blida to rejoin the squadon. The next day the remaining aircrews and ground personnel arrived at Blida.

On 6th August 1943 the main party consisting of aircrew and essential maintenance personnel, around 92 staff, left Blida and arrived at Protville in squadron aircraft. A maintenance party of 56 also left Blida. On 8th August 1943 the main party of 161 squadron personnel left Blida by raid. On 22nd August the squadron moved to Bizelta, Sicily. The Evening Gazette noted on November 15th 1943 "Teesside's Own Flying Men Celebrate Overseas, pointing out that 608 Squadron was celebrating its first birthday overseas. After more than three years operating from English and Scottish stations, the squadron left home last November believing that they were to do convoy duties over the South Atlantic. They touched down at Gibraltar and there late at night were let into the great secret. In a few hours they were informed by a Group Captaiin, the Allies would land in North Africa. Flying Hudsons, the squadron gradually moved east – Algeria, Tunisia and Sicily. In Italy they escorted convoys when our troops were battling in the critical operation at Salerno."

Throughout July 1944 squadron personnel and aircraft were being posted out. On 22nd July 1944 official instructions were received for a reduction of 608 Squadron to a numbers basis. On 26th July the squadron trophies, that was 2 propellers, the squadron crest, shields and an official squadron history and pictorial record were forwarded to the Station Commander RAF Thornaby for safe keeping until the end of the war. On 27th July at Pomigliano the squadron numbers were reduced to 4 officers, 4 senior NCOs and 19 airmen. On 31st July 1944 all equipment and vehicles were handed over and all personnel dismissed. After 14 years No 608 (NR) Squadron was disbanded. There, 608 Squadrons job was to photograph ports, escort ships, and most importantly, to destroy enemy submarines. They moved along the coast and on into Italy until on 1st April 1944 the squadron was disbanded from Pomigliano, largely because most of the officers and aircrew were no longer auxiliary men. The Squadron's trophies, i.e. two propellers, the Squadron crest, shields and other official squadron history were forwarded to the Station Commander at RAF Station Thornaby for safe keeping until the end of the war. The Squadron was reformed the next day as a Mosquito Bomber Squadron.

A Selection of Veterans Photographs

Mr John Pollock's Collection

Mr John Pollock's Collection

Mr John Pollock's Collection

Mr P Vaux's Collection

Mr P Vaux's Collection

Mr P Vaux's Collection

Mr P Vaux's Collection

Mr P Vaux's Collection

Mr P Vaux's Collection

Mr P Vaux's Collection

L Wilkinson's Collection

1946-1957
Re-formed at Thornaby

The Auxiliary Air Force was reconstituted on 10th May 1946. It was initially located within Reserve Command; this meant that all the Auxiliary units were lumped together with the RAFVR, the University Air Squadrons and the Air Training Corps. However, the AAF squadrons did not start to re-form until June and July of that year, and 608 Squadron was reformed as part of No 64 Group Reserve Command equipped initially with Mosquito aircraft N F 30 (coded RAO) and Oxford T2 (Coded 6T RAO). By 1948, all AAF squadrons had been integrated into Fighter Command as Day Fighter Units.

On 15th November 1946 adverts were placed in local newspapers to start the recruitment process for officers and airmen in the post-war 608 Squadron. One advert stated those ex-servicemen who missed the spirit of comradeship which existed in the services during the World War will find it again by joining the Auxiliary Air Force. A similar advert stated recruiting for the above Squadron had commenced and there were still a limited number of vacancies for officers (Aircrew and General Duties) and airmen (Aircrew and Ground Duties). Enlistment was confined to ex-members of the Royal Air Force. The Yorkshire Post commented, Recruiting for the new Auxiliary Air Force of 20 flying squadrons opens tomorrow and will be carried out by the individual squadrons the Air Ministry announces. At present only officers and men who have served with the Air Force during the war are eligible to join. Vacancies exist for flying members, for personnel for ground trades and for technical, medical, administrative and equipment duties. These points are interesting. In the first instance only ex RAF personnel were being encouraged to join the squadron and secondly the advertisements focus on the spirit of comradeship as a means of interesting ex servicemen to apply to join.

By 4th December 1946 ninety applications had been received for various vacancies that had been advertised within 608 Squadron. This meant that by 31st December 18 tradesmen and 4 air-crew had been enlisted and eleven applications for officers had been submitted to the Air Ministry for approval. On 18th January 1947 Squadron Leader William Appleby-Brown was gazetted as CO of 608 Squadron with effect from 1st August 1946. He had been a member of 608 Squadron since October 1937 with a distinguished flying career throughout the war. On appointment, the local press confirmed his connections to the locality of Teesside by noting that in civilian life, he and his brother worked in the Middlesbrough firm of J.W. Brown and Co Ltd, Shipbrokers and Merchants. Following the selection of the new CO, on 15th November 1946, adverts were placed in both local and national newspapers to start the recruitment process not just for airmen but also officers, and this in itself represented a new approach to recruitment. Some of the adverts concentrated on particular areas that might appeal to potential volunteers; for example, it was suggested that those ex-servicemen who missed the spirit of comradeship that had existed in the services during the World War would rediscover it again by joining the Auxiliary Air Force. A severe snowfall led to the station being placed on a care and maintenance basis in order to conserve fuel. Recruiting was also held up due to the bad weather.

In 1947, the recruiting regulations changed and a local paper stated, recruits were to consist of ex-RAF personnel, but this stipulation had been reconsidered and, in future, anybody who had been released from the Services would be considered. The first summer camp for the Squadron took place at Thornaby with exercises taking place over Germany and Holland. Employers have given their full co-operation, and the time spent at camp would be in addition to the customary summer holidays. Another interesting point is that former RAF personnel, who wanted to join 608 Squadron, or any other auxiliary squadron, were prepared to drop rank in order to be accepted. This point is reinforced by a local newspaper which stated self-evident is the happy camaraderie which animates all ranks and one of the first things I noticed at the YMCA, was that among the throng clamouring for a "cupper tea and a wad" was a sergeant pilot wearing the ribbon of the DFC, an indication that he had dropped rank in order to rejoin. He is not alone in that respect. The CO, Squadron Leader W Appleby-Brown DFC, was formerly a Wing Commander and there are many others who have readily shed a "ring" or a "crown" or exchanged "galloping horses" for chevrons in order to get back. This comment was typical of the comments passed by veterans that were interviewed.

However, this new openness did not lead to a rush of recruits. Increased technical demands and a more rigorous selection process served to keep numbers down. The recruitment process was much more carefully controlled and acceptance into the AAF took much longer than it had before the war when status equated to acceptance. Consequently, in conjunction with most of the other AAF squadrons, 608 Squadron struggled to recruit sufficient personnel to reach their establishment, in fact, by July 1947, it had only 12 officers and 44 airmen enlisted which amounted to 25% of the station establishment.

Another significant factor in slowing down recruitment was the conditions of service, which required the attendance for twelve weekends and fifteen days at annual camp, as well as the completion of one hundred hours of 'non-continuous' training. Many potential recruits could not meet this level of commitment. Aircrews were slightly different in that they were expected to put in one hundred and twenty five hours flying a year. Volunteers had to be prepared to commit to the conditions of service and therefore had to be willing to give up a significant amount of their free time in order to fulfil their obligations to the AAF. Slow recruiting across the country prompted the Air Ministry to change the recruiting regulations in 1947, but the number of potential recruits slowed down considerably as many men felt that they had served their time during the war, had made the most of their opportunities to work with aircraft and satisfied their desire for travel. In a more expansive modern world, the opportunities that the AAF offered young men were not as appealing as they had been in the 1930s, because there were now new chances to travel or work in more challenging environments in civilian life.

Recruiting by the end of March 1948 was at 39% of the establishment figures for the Royal Auxiliary Air Force across the country. National attention turned to new conscripts who were being compelled by the National Service Act of 1948, to join H.M. Forces. Initially the time period of national service was eighteen months but this was extended to two years following the outbreak of the Korean War. An agreement was made that 300 National Service conscripts would be selected for flying training each year and these men would fulfil their subsequent reserve obligation by either becoming members of the Volunteer Reserve, or of an auxiliary squadron. In this way it was hoped that the poor numbers of recruits for the AAF squadrons could be boosted. This change in policy would benefit recruitment to 608 Squadron.

Most of the post-war recruits wanted to pursue their interest in aircraft and maintain the comradeship of the war. They were able to maintain their civilian jobs, receive a small second income as a member of the AAF and enjoy weekend camps and summer camps. Respondents in 608 Squadron and other squadrons talked of it making their lives more enjoyable, enabling them to have some structure within their leisure time, fulfilling their interest in aircraft, and giving them a sense of pride in both country and local community.

Viscount Swinton remained as 608 Squadron's Honorary Air Commodore after the war and continued to be the only real link to the upper middle class backgrounds of the pre-war officers who had served within the squadron. Although the employment backgrounds of the officers were different, the backgrounds of post-war airmen remained similar to their pre-war contemporaries. All of the men interviewed felt that their employers in civilian life approved and actively encouraged them to join. Furthermore, all the veterans felt a strong sense of patriotism in the aftermath of the Second World War.

It is apparent that there was a mellowing of relations between 608 Squadron and the local community in the years following the end of World War II. Clearly, the pre-war lack of interest in any military activity or organisation following World War I led to public apathy and a tense relationship between the two groups as opposed to the wave of patriotism which swept England following the end of the Second World War. This manifestation of a more positive relationship can be seen in a number of ways.

During World War II bonds were built between the Aerodrome and the local community through several different activities. Football matches between NCOs and airmen were popular and on Christmas Day in 1942, a match was played at Ayresome Park, the old home of

Middlesbrough Football Club, between an Allied Air Force XI and Middlesbrough Police which was watched by over 5,000 spectators. Another way of building bridges with locals was through collaborative fund raising activities; the "Spitfire Fund" was set up on 21st August 1940 by the people of Billingham, Stockton and Thornaby. There were a variety of different activities used to raise money including flag days, and the 'mile of pennies', which were laid down by members of the public who had been persuaded by the Auxiliary Fire Service. Another idea raised £20 when the Maison de Dance forfeited one night's takings. This improvement in relations between 608 Squadron and its local community was fostered largely because each was facing a "common enemy", but there was a continuation of the improved relationship once the war ended.

In the first instance, the "at home" days of the pre-war era continued after 1945 when the Aerodrome was opened to the public to watch air displays and to take guided tours, meet staff and see aircraft at close quarters. The main purpose was to build close links between the aerodrome and community. Post-war patriotism led to increased interest in celebratory occasions to remember Britain's struggle during the war, a war which had affected local civilian populations in a much more profound way than the First World War. These days were often tied to the Battle of Britain Memorial Days which took place across the country and which encouraged a wider range of people to visit the aerodrome. Initially these "at home" days were also used as a means to attract new recruits and to develop interest amongst the younger generation who would be able to see the new jet aircraft at close quarters, talk to existing staff about their different jobs and finding out about opportunities for careers within either the AAF or the RAF.

Recruiting posters were posted throughout the local area, and regular notifications of staff shortages were placed in newspapers in an effort to raise the local profile of the squadron. Moreover, officers from 608 Squadron visited local cinemas and dance halls with posters and leaflets explaining the benefits of being a member.

Squadron dances took place after the war. John Pollock remembers "the girls used to pay 3s 6d to go into the dance hall and the AAF chaps went in for nothing. When we were building the memorial, lots of women came up to me and said how they remembered having such a good time up there at the dances." The squadron dances took place in the Drill Hall on a Thursday night and entertainment was provided by Jim Gardener and his band. Local girls "were conveyed from Stockton Town Hall in double-decker buses, courtesy of RAF Thornaby."

The Squadron always managed to be involved in local events, such as the Remembrance Parade, the local football championships and cricket matches; its band was very popular, and weekly squadron dances were a valuable public relations exercise as well as a source of recreation. The squadron also had its own aerobatic team which would travel around airfields in the North East putting on displays. Much of the tension that had existed between the local community and the aerodrome in the 1930s had all but disappeared in these latter days.

Auxiliary Air Force personnel for 608 Squadron in January 1947 were one officer with 13 awaiting gazettement and 31 airmen. By the middle of March 1947, other officers included Flight Lieutenant J Hodgson DFC, Flying Officer T Willis, Flight Lieutenant G G Wood, Flying Officer A Gavan, Flying Instructor P Grant and Flight Lieutenant H W Oliver. On 12th April 1947 full AAF training commenced at Thornaby with 2 Oxfords and 2 Mosquito's. Squadron strength was 10 officers and 31 airmen including new officer commissions for Flying Officers J D Turnbull, T Appleton and J Crawford. Squadron aircraft strength stood at 3 Oxfords and 3 Mosquito's.

In May 1947 the Squadron underwent weekend training visited by Vice Marshal Sir Alan Lees Commander in Chief Reserve Command, and this was followed by a further visit from Sir Alan Lees with Air Commodore BV Reynolds to inspect the squadron and take the salute. The Northern Echo of July 11th 1947 noted that "a flying start has been made by 608 Auxiliary Air Squadron at Thornaby with recruiting and training, and with 12 officers and 44 airmen now enlisted, the squadron shows the highest returns for all Northern Command Reserve Squadrons." This was followed in August of the same year with the annual camp including flying exercises over Germany and Holland. These activities were widely reported in the local press. In October 1947, Squadron strength had risen to 12 officers, 8 airmen aircrew and 44 tradesmen with 2 Mosquito XXX, 5 Mosquito III and 3 Oxfords. A year later 3 Harvard and 13 Spitfire's were also added to the aircraft strength of the squadron and this was further increased by the end of 1949, when squadron strength stood at 10 officers and 120 airmen, with 14 Spitfire's, 13 Harvard's and 1 Oxford. Christmas Eve 1947 saw 608 Squadron holding a Christmas party for local children and a twin engine plane was "put at the disposal of the old gentleman by Squadron Leader Appleby-Brown. Pilot, Flight Lieutenant J McAllister, DFC, safely delivered his VIP to the wild excitement of the 80 youngsters."

Saturday 18th September 1948 saw 15,000 spectators enjoying an "at home" day at Thornaby. The North Eastern Daily News noted that "From 15,000 gaping mouths came a gasp of aspiration as a silver streak flashing by at 600 miles an hour, climbed steeply into the blue to execute a perfect loop. Going through its paces was a Meteor III jet fighter, one of the latest and fastest additions to Britain's air strength." Later that year the Squadron converted to the Spiffire F22.

On 19 September 1949, services to commemorate the Battle of Britain were held across the country. A service was held at the Cenotaph Middlesbrough. The ceremony of the laying of the wreath was performed by Squadron Leader J T Shaw DSO, DFC, Officer Commanding the Thornaby Unit accompanied by Flight Lieutenant G T Williams OBE DFM On the 11th May Squadron Leader F A Robinson DFC became CO of 608 Squadron and the de Havilland Vampire F3 jet fighters arrived. In July of the same year 608 Squadron attended annual camp at Horsham St Faith near Norwich. The whole unit comprising of 20 officers and 105 other ranks under command of Squadron Leader F A Robinson made the trip by air. The ground crews went by RAF transport aircraft and the pilots went by Vampires in which they had recently converted. The jet aircraft made the trip in less than forty minutes. The establishment also included a Meteor T7 and a Harvard T26.

On 18th September 1949 services to commemorate the Battle of Britain were held across the country. The local service was held at the Cenotaph in Middlesbrough. The ceremony of the laying of the wreath was performed by Squadron Leader J T Shaw DSO, DFC, Officer Commanding the Thornaby Unit accompanied by Flight Lieutenant G T Williams OBE DFM.

On 11th may 1950 Squadron Leader F A Robinson DFC became Officer Commanding No 608 Squadron, and in July of that year, the squadron attended annual camp at Horsham St Faith near Norwich. The whole unit comprising of 20 officers and 105 other ranks made the trip by air. The ground crews went by RAF transport aircraft and the pilots flew their Vampires in which they had recently converted. The jet aircraft made the trip in less than 40 minutes. The Vampire jets were Mark F3 and FB5 (coded 6T0 and the establishment included a Meteor T7 and a Harvard T26 9coded 6T0. On 16th September 1950 the anniversary celebration of the Battle of Britain at Thornaby took place. Large crowds made their way to the aerodrome in buses, cars on bicycles and on foot in time for the opening fanfare by the band of the 17/21 Lancers. A full afternoon's entertainment was offered including formation flying by Vampire jets and Tiger Moths. Later in the afternoon there was the "set piece" bombing of aircraft and hangers in which warning was given of the approach of enemy aircraft and the taking off of defending fighters. In addition to these air displays there were sideshows and static displays by other units of the RAF. This event continued in September of each year.

In May 1950 the squadron went to Aclington for different types of training and the strength of the unit was 15 officers and 153 airmen. Reports in the press noted that "the weekend airmen of 608 squadron Royal Auxiliary Air Force were converting to jet fighters – Vampires and Meteors and whilst visiting them, Lieutenant Colonel M J B Burnett, DSO, secretary of the North Riding Territorial Association watched an impressive display of four of the jet fighters taking off to intercept an American Super-fortress flying in from the sea at over 25,000 feet."

However, there was some apprehension on the part of the local authority regarding the ability of the aerodrome to cope with technologically-advanced jet aircraft that were becoming more familiar during the late 1940s. Questions were raised about the location of the aerodrome and the impact on surrounding housing. The *Northern Echo* raised their concerns in May 1947 when it suggested that

> the future of Thornaby RAF Aerodrome might well be reviewed because of the restrictive effect it is having on new housing. The Air Ministry announced some time ago that it was re-establishing an auxiliary squadron on the station but it is doubtful if the airfield now meets the needs of most of modern operational aircraft.

The comment was refuted the next day by William Appleby-Brown, Squadron CO, who stated "it would appear that the writer is somewhat misinformed about the airfield at Thornaby. At present it is quite suitable for modern operational aircraft and Mosquitos are now being flown by this squadron."

However, the suggestion that AAF stations and personnel were not equipped to fly modern fighter planes was a common complaint voiced right across the country, and raised wider concerns about the efficiency of the Auxiliary Air Force. Undoubtedly the technological advances that were being made in aircraft design meant that auxiliary squadrons sometimes struggled to maintain proficiency when compared to regular personnel. This factor prompted the government to analyse the competence of the part-time personnel, and it was these concerns that ultimately led to the winding down of the AAF in 1957.

Empire air day from John Pollock's collection

15th September 1951 saw Battle of Britain Day at the aerodrome. Thousands of visitors including crowds of schoolboys descended on Thornaby RAF Station for the "At Home" activities. Owing to unfavourable weather at the start of the afternoon, the first two flying events on the programme, a take off by Vampires of 608 Squadron and a fly past of Washington heavy bombers was postponed. There was a lot of interest in the static display of aircraft which included a D H Vampire, a Gloster Meteor, a Harvard, an Avro Lincoln, a D H Mosquito, a Miles Marburet and a Hawker Tempest. Also open for inspection by the visitors were the living and dining quarters of the airmen and airwomen, the station sick quarters and the concert hall.

Air Display at Thornaby C. 1950

FLT-LT. WILLIS

'608' PILOT KILLED ON WAY HOME

A 29-YEAR-OLD Middlesbrough jet fighter-pilot was killed yesterday when his Vampire plane crashed at Eloouina Airport, near Tunis, as he was returning to this country with other members of the 608 (North Riding) Royal Auxiliary Air Force Squadron who are based at Thornaby.

The pilot was Flt-Lt. Thomas Allan Willis, of 71, The Avenue, Linthorpe. Willis and other members of the squadron he had landed in Tunisia to re-fuel on the journey back to Thornaby from Malta, where the squadron has been training for the past fortnight.

Flight-Lieut. Willis, the son of Mr. and Mrs. Allan Willis, of 61, Devonshire-road, Middlesbrough was employed by the I.C.I. at Billingham in the export department.

An old boy of Acklam Hall Grammar School, he was a fighter pilot during the war and flew Spitfires, Typhoons and Tempests without injury in various parts of the world.

In April 1947, he was commissioned in the 608 Squadron of the Royal Auxiliary Air Force.

He is married.

Mrs Willis (Sister of Allan Willis) Collection

In 1952 the Vampire F3 jets were replaced by the Vampire FB5 and Squadron Leader G A Martin, DFC, AFC, RAF became Commanding Officer. On 12th September 1952 Flt Lt Thomas Alan Willis was killed returning a plane from 608 Squadron's summer camp at Ta Kali in Malta. He had been commissioned in 608 Squadron in 1947, the son of Mr and Mrs Albert Willis of Middlesbrough. He was 29 years old and was married. His Vampire plane crashed at Elaouina airport near Tunis as he was returning to Britain with other members of the 608 squadron. He had landed in Tunisia to refuel on the journey back to Thornaby. Employed by ICI at Billingham in the Export Department and an old boy of Acklam Hall Grammar School, he was a fighter pilot during the war. He flew Spitfires, Typhoons and Tempests without injury in several parts of the world.

Mrs Willis Collection

From Left to Right
Flight Lieutenant Hector Watts, Pilot Officer Allen Clough, Master Pilot Bill
Sykens, Flight Lieutenant Bill Goodrum, unknown, Flying Officer Ken Temple,
Flying Officer Bill Swainston, Squadron Leader George Martin (Commanding
Officer 608 Squadron) and Flying Officer Allan Willis.

Mrs Willis Collection

On the 18th September a memorial service took place for Flight
Lieutenant Willis. The lesson was read by Squadron Leader Martin,
Squadron CO. Among those present were Group Captain G Shaw
and Wing Commander M K Sewell, CO of RAF Thornaby.

On 20th September 1952 the Battle of Britain Day took place again at
the aerodrome. Although conditions were far from ideal a crowd of
several thousand saw the programme of flying events. The display
was part of an "at home" at the aerodrome to commemorate the 12th
anniversary of the Battle of Britain. The heads of most local
authorities on Teesside attended. Formation flying by four Vampire
fighters of 608 Squadron flown by Squadron Leader G H Martin,
Flight Lieutenant W Goodrum and Pilot Officers A Clough and W
Swainson opened the display. Shortly after the display began, Air
Vice Marshall R L Atcherley Officer commanding Fighter Group
arrived in a Meteor. Some of the jet aircraft had to hunt around in

cloud before finding a clear patch in which to perform. Visitors also saw a static display of aircraft and equipment. They could also visit a barrack block and the airman' dining hall.

Another Battle of Britain Day took place on 19th September 1953. Thornaby Aerodrome with its thousands of visitors had the appearance of a miniature Farnborough. The fine weather gave prospects of a record crowd and the show opened with four of the latest type Vampire Jets flashing over the runway in a low level flypast hover plane display. One of the latest types of Sycamore helicopter was put through its paces. An American Salve jet fighter from the 2nd Tactical Air Force in Germany was to attempt to break through the sound barrier. Altogether nearly 50 aricraft were taking part including three Canberra jet bombers. Among those present was Viscount Swinton, Honourary Air Commodore of the three auxiliary units at Thornaby. Air Commander R L Kippen AOC No 64 Group, Squadron Leader F G Daw, Station Commander, Squadron Leader G W H Ware, Officer Commanding RAF Cold Hesledon, the Mayor and Mayoresses of Middlesbrough, Stockton, Thornaby, Hartlepool and West Hartlepool were also present. Lord Swinton took the salute at the exhibition of continuous drill given by an RAF Regiment team from Catterick. Among other items was a demonstration of crazy flying by Tiger Moths, a demonstration of glider towing and a flypast by Sunderland Flying Boats, a ground attack exercise by eight Vampires and a formation drill by Vampires.

However, an RAF Regiment man died when a truck overturned on the perimeter track at the airfield after he had crossed the main runway and approached a slight bend.

Newspaper reports from October 1954 showed that Middlesbrough had adopted Royal Air Force Station Thornaby as part of an idea being fostered by the Air Ministry. The idea being for Municipal Corporations to have a municipal liaison scheme under which certain RAF stations are affiliated to neighbouring cities and towns.

This year saw renewed complaints from local residents about flying at the Aerodrome. Some suggested that low flying aircraft had endangered the lives of patients in Stockton and Thornaby Hospital and the Commander in Chief of Fighter Command had promised "vigorous action" to minimise such disturbances." 1954 Thornaby revived its wartime air-sea rescue role when 275 Squadron arrived in

November from Linton - on - Ouse. They were equipped with Sycamore helicopters and were engaged on search and rescue duties along the North East Coast. In 1955 Squadron Leader H D Costain became Commanding Officer of 608 Squadron and the Squadron received Vampire FB9 jets. Major changes took place in 1957 when in March 608 Squadron disbanded along with all other units of the Royal Auxiliary Air Force.

Officers and Airmen

When 608 Squadron reformed in 1946, the format for activities was much the same as before the war. Again the men would attend for one or two evenings a week and then on a Saturday and a Sunday. Pilots flew nearly all the time, specifically undertaking target practice. Here a training plane, usually a Meteor, took off towing a drogue, a large target which stayed upright in the air. The planes from 608 squadron would have specific flying slots throughout the weekend. They would take off and fire ammunition-containing dye at the drogue. When their slot was finished, they would return to Thornaby, and the Meteor plane would fly over the airfield and drop the drogue. The drogue would then be pulled into the hanger and the accuracy of the pilots shooting could be seen. The worst-case scenario was if one of the pilots shot the wires holding the drogue and the drogue was lost. This could waste hours of time while a new Meteor was found to pull another drogue. The planes would come down and would be checked and serviced before taking off again. Many of the pilots attended the aerodrome each night to keep their flying hours up, especially during the summer months.

On the evenings, dances were often held at the aerodrome attended by both the airmen and the local girls. Many of the 608 airmen married local girls. Other recreational activities included the cinema at Thornaby, or Stockton, and of course the dance halls in Stockton, Middlesbrough and Redcar. The location of Thornaby to the railway station was of course a bonus. Men often went to the Odd Fellows Arms, nicknamed "The Odd Bods", but many considered that it was too near the camp; after all it was located directly opposite the guardroom. That meant that if a problem occurred, the men could be collected and brought back to work.

The occupations of volunteers for officer posts in the reformed AAF were different from those of the pre-war officers. Many men worked for ICI undertaking a variety of skilled jobs including draughtsman

97

(Jim Steedman), metallurgist (Harry Bates), analyst (George Joyce), and researcher (Grant Goodwill). All these jobs involved technical training and knowledge and reflected the higher emphasis that was being placed on skill and intelligence in English post-war society, as well as within military institutions. It also demonstrated the fact that technical knowledge did not necessarily have to be acquired through a traditional public-school and university education but could be learned through experience or other forms of training. Other officer volunteers in the post-war 608 Squadron came from a wider range of occupational backgrounds: Bill Goodrum ran his own building business. Jim Marshall and Dave Stewart worked at Dorman Long, Bill Swainston was an engineer, Alan Clough worked for the Electricity Board and Hank Hancock worked for British Rail.

Many of the men now came from the large corporate industries such as ICI and this impacted on the relationships that existed between all ranks because many officers and lower ranks knew each other within their civilian jobs. Furthermore, only a small minority of officers, such as William Appleby-Brown, continued to work within family businesses. Large companies were happy to support such voluntarism and often contributed significantly to the needs of the community as part of a wider paternalistic approach to industrial relations.

Many ex-service men found it hard to adapt to civilian jobs and life and felt they lacked the interaction and teamwork that had characterised life in the RAF. Jim Steedman put it bluntly, "we didn't enjoy our jobs so that's why we joined." Grant Goodwill enjoyed being in the AAF more than his civilian job at ICI and noted' "I nearly got the sack from ICI for taking too much time off." George Joyce also gave up his shift work in the labs at ICI to become a full time auxiliary with his friends Hancock and Mackenzie: "we were working five days a week and flying Saturdays, Sundays and Thursday nights. We were shattered, drinking like idiots, partying and after six months of this we decided something had got to give, so we gave our jobs up."

Those who had flown with the Royal Air Force during the war could effectively be offered positions within the AAF as officers, based on their technical skills and regardless of their background and social status. Ted Brown caught the new mood:

Before the war most pilots were officers and it didn't matter whether you had brains or not, you would fly the aircraft. The officers weren't the brightest by any means, and often it was your family relationship that got you your position. It wasn't the case after the war; the fittest and the brightest became pilots.

Many of the post-war officers had served in the squadron prior to the war and were prepared to accept a substantial reduction in rank in order to rejoin. This initial willingness to enlist in the AAF was reflected across the country and highlights the wave of post-war patriotism that swept Britain. This can be seen in the case of Mr Winstanley who, having served in the regular RAF, joined 608 Squadron in 1946 and "had to drop two ranks from Warrant Officer pilot in the regular RAF to Sergeant pilot in 608 Squadron." David Stewart also served with 608 Squadron between 1949 and 1952 and was an officer during his time in the RAF but had to re-join 608 Squadron as a Warrant Officer pilot flying spitfires and vampires. Other former RAF personnel, who wanted to join 608 Squadron, were prepared to drop rank in order to be accepted. A local reporter who met a sergeant pilot wearing the ribbon of the DFC reinforced this point noting that this was an indication that he had dropped rank in order to rejoin. John Pollock also served as a Sergeant in the RAF but dropped three ranks to be an AC2 when he joined 608 Squadron.

However, of those veterans interviewed who had served in 608 Squadron during the 1930s and the war, many felt that they had "done their bit" and that they did not want to rejoin the AAF after the war. Flying was no longer a novelty, it was no longer a sport, it was an accepted symbol of modernity and therefore had in some ways, lost its appeal. Whilst the initial level of interest was overwhelming, the actual number of men who met the criteria for enlisting was disappointing and reflected the new recruitment restrictions placed on all squadrons. Selection of officers, NCOs and airmen was now much more demanding, with particular emphasis on previous experience and knowledge. These demands were relaxed in 1948 to allow any ex-service-men to join the Auxiliary Air Force in an effort to increase recruitment. However, in many ways this action was too late to enable the AAF squadrons to benefit from the immediate post-war wave of enthusiasm which subsequently waned as men successfully re-adapted to civilian life.

Interviews with respondents reveal that reasons for joining the post-war AAF were wide and varied. Officer recruits such as Geoffrey Milburn noted that there was "a small item called conscription, plus a family RAF tradition." Jim Steedman volunteered for 608 Squadron after completing his national service. George Joyce noted that following his demob from national service he volunteered for 608 Squadron because "the social side of squadron life was an attraction," while Grant Goodwill, who followed the same route noted that "access to flying and aircraft" was the main incentive for his decision to volunteer. On the other hand, Ted Brown gave several reasons for volunteering: "joining 608 Squadron gave me the opportunity to visit other countries, to be with my friends, to receive pay from the AAF and from ICI and that meant that my life was like a holiday."

Norman Winstanley served in the RAF during the war and stated

> the transition from service life was terrible, to suddenly leave all your pals. Because there was a tremendous spirit. In fact, I was so desperate I was thinking about going back in, and then I saw an advert in the *Gazette* for volunteers for 608 Squadron. I was off to the aerodrome like a shot.

For all the new openness in terms of recruitment, social activities within 608 Squadron after the Second World War continued to be based upon rank and position. The mess structure within the forces meant that officers had their own mess, as did sergeants whilst the airmen had the NAAFI. This hierarchical structure meant that officers and men were still kept separate and this resulted in specific locations where each group of men would go to socialise. Even after the war, the officers kept to themselves. They did not mix with the NCOs unless there was a function in the Sergeants' mess that they were specifically invited to attend. Similarly the officers did not mix with the men, nor did the NCOs. Indeed Jim Steedman noted, the system of separate messes was standard RAF practice. Most of the men interviewed socialised in the Odd Fellows Arms, a public house that was located just opposite the guardroom of Thornaby Aerodrome. The officers who were interviewed tended to socialise in Yarm, in the Pathfinders at Maltby, The Pot and Glass at Eaglescliffe, The Vane Arms in Stockton, the cocktail bar upstairs in the Odd Fellows Arms or the officers' mess. Most of the officers interviewed mentioned the pranks and behaviour that were still part and parcel of life in the officer's mess. Drinking and playing games by the younger officers were part of everyday life; When asked about socialising Grant Goodwill described a typical night of socialising,

"There was a certain code of behaviour in the mess. It wasn't loutish behaviour. Everybody had a good drink, I must admit that. We always used to end up at the officers mess, unless there was a special dance on or a party, you never go down to the mess early doors. You would either go down the Oddies, the Odd Fellows that was the local pub; they had a cocktail bar upstairs. Then you would end up down in Stockton. We would go to the Maison and the Palais, the dance halls that were there, and then you would end up back, sometimes in time for the last drink at the Oddies, and then head back to the mess around eleven o' clock. That's why we ended up drinking until two o' clock; we never got there till at least eleven."

When asked about the social mix of officers and airmen at the Odd Fellows he stated,

"well strangely enough, the airmen would be downstairs. We would be in the cocktail bar upstairs. You would never get the airmen up there you see. We used to go up and drink upstairs. We didn't consciously keep out of the way of the airmen; they probably kept out of our way. They had their own places to go and drink."

George Joyce pointed out,

"we had one or two sergeant pilots on the squadron and of course we had a different mess from them, but all of the squadron were treated as equals. The mess was relatively formal. Everybody behaved in a pleasant way, you were expected to conform to certain basic rules, and you never talked about sex, religion or politics in the mess. You had to eat with the right knife and fork. It was not like the RAF. We had formal dining-ins where you had to get all dressed up and toast the Queen, but it always finished up with mess games. Being an auxiliary there was a certain element of disregard for the regulars. There was lots of horseplay; there was very little formality."

He noted, "Several of us had cars. If we met the airmen we would say "hi," to them but I suppose subconsciously you would tend to veer away from the places they frequented really. The main contact we had with them was down on the flight."

Social life within the squadron held a certain masculine appeal for both officers and airmen, although it is evident from the interviews that the officers appear to have placed greater importance on social activities in the mess than the airmen. Many of the airmen who were interviewed did not stay on the aerodrome over the weekend because they lived locally and preferred to go home to their families once they had completed their daily tasks. They were quite happy to report for duty the next morning, although a number of airmen interviewed did call into the Odd Fellows Arms for a drink or two before going home. Significantly alcohol and social activity played a much more important role for the officers than it did for the men. The officers functioned in a completely different way socially within the officers' mess and within the local public houses that they frequented. In the main they still continued to engage in public school boy antics in both social settings; however the mess games were a major part of weekend activities especially amongst the younger pilots, and it is clear that the older officers would retire to another room to enable the younger element to "let off steam".

All of the officers interviewed were clear about the lack of social mixing between themselves and the airmen, and most noted that separation of ranks was a normal part of military life. However, it is apparent that during the two weeks annual camp, when the squadron travelled abroad for training, there was a much more relaxed relationship between the officers and the men and a greater likelihood of the two groups mixing. This was not seen as unacceptable because the camp was meant to be a combination of work and play where the rules of everyday life in the squadron were temporarily suspended. Class and rank were transcended during this holiday period by a common sense of national identity in a foreign context. Bob Harbron noted,

> "When we went to places like Germany or Malta or Gibraltar, we were ambassadors. We were sort of flying the flag; more than the regular air force, because we were half way, we were civilian and military. It was pride, pride in the organisation."

Ted Brown also supports this view

> "Most nights we tended to go out. But you might have arranged

to go to a certain place, and the officers might have arranged to go to the same place. But there was no demarcation. Everyone sat and everybody chatted to each other and had a laugh and a giggle. Everyone just mixed together when we were in Malta."

Bob Harbron remembered the more relaxed relationship between officers and men on summer camp: "If you were in Valetta and you all turned up at the same bar, then you would all sit together and have a drink. This wouldn't have happened in the regular RAF." Jim Steedman had much the same story to tell: "if you saw the lads out when you were out on a weekend exercise away, you would meet up with the lads and have a drink together." Clearly a different relationship existed between officers and men when away from the aerodrome, and reinforces the point that class relationships were dynamic and never entirely fixed. Thus the context within which the officers and airmen met created different relationships. For example, class barriers were less apparent during the war itself because all were united against the common external enemy. Once the war ended, the military hierarchy relationships reasserted themselves, but the annual summer camp brought commonality to the fore. Officers and airmen mixed more readily because of the concept of the "gentleman abroad".

When considering the relationships between officers and men, Alan Huitson claimed that there was a "friendly positive relationship with no divide." Several men noted that all people on the aerodrome worked together as a team and each had their own part to play. The officers were aware of the role that the airmen played and vice versa. Ted Brown, on the other hand, felt that the only real contact between the officers and the airmen was through flying, whereas Bob Harbron said "We knew them outside the AAF, we knew them as bank managers, chemists, solicitors; we knew them at that level. We knew they were working the same as us."

He also made clear his belief that

an auxiliary squadron it was white and grey. That was the feel of everybody. They knew that on Monday we would all be going back to work, we would all be getting on the bus, we'd all be wondering what sort of job we were going to get this week and it didn't, if anything it gave more of a caring squadron as opposed to a Royal Air Force disciplinary squadron. And we all knew each other. That was the main thing. We knew each other's foibles and we knew where each other worked and we didn't take advantage of it, in fact we sort of helped each other along regarding it.

Interestingly enough some respondents thought there was more of a problem elsewhere in the squadron; as Alan Huitson recollects, "there was a noticeable divide between the NCOs and us." This view is supported by Malcolm Ruecroft who said that "sometimes NCOs and airmen did not get on well. We had more contact with the NCOs and the rank structure meant that they disciplined us." Both Grant Goodwill and George Joyce, who were pilots in the reformed AAF, stated that the NCOs and airmen had more contact with each other and that this relationship was therefore more liable to be fractious. The officers tended to only have contact with the men and the NCOs when they were actually flying, and appeared to have a more positive affiliation because they relied so heavily upon the ground crews to ensure that their aircraft were safe.

All men who were interviewed felt that there was a positive relationship between the regular RAF and the 608 Squadron. Bob Harbron noted "the balance between the regulars and the auxiliaries was very good because most of the auxiliaries of 1950 had seen war service." Furthermore Ted Brown stated "we were all there to do a job really, it didn't matter what they called you, you did a job and there was no differentiation between us." Jim Steedman said that "the relationship was excellent, but there was not much contact because the AAF lads replaced the regular men when they were in." George Crow noted "on the squadrons you did your work – you were more or less the same;" whilst Malcolm Ruecroft felt "it was okay. Yes. There was never any of that "part-timers." I never heard anything like that." George Joyce said, "being an auxiliary there was a certain element of disregard for the regulars. There was lots of horseplay, there was very little formality." The regular RAF personnel at Thornaby had the job of running the aerodrome throughout the week and were responsible for its day-to-day functioning. The auxiliaries worked alongside the regulars on a weekend and during the summer camp and during these times, the two depended upon each other to ensure that everything ran smoothly. The arrival of the auxiliaries on a weekend meant that the regulars were able to have time off and relax. The regular RAF personnel were also responsible for training the AAF staff and therefore it was essential that they were able to develop positive relationships with them.

When asked about the skills that the men gained from being part of 608 Squadron, both Grant Goodwill and George Joyce felt that they were able to build upon their flying experience gained during the war, which enabled them to become commercial pilots once the AAF disbanded in 1957. Many of the men were able to build on their technical skills in armaments and explosive training, electrical skills, instrument handling and driving. All noted that they gained supervisory skills and learned to handle responsibility, which improved their prospects in civilian life. The men also learned to accept discipline and to work as part of a team with a variety of people from different backgrounds. All of the men who were interviewed had a strong national identity and sense of patriotism. They believed that they had a duty to defend their country and were proud to wear a uniform and be part of the AAF. Most of the men are still very patriotic and would rejoin the AAF if the opportunity arose.

There is evidence of both change and continuity here, in terms of change, we can certainly see a more open policy towards recruitment within the AAF nationally, yet this new openness still fed into a distinct military hierarchy where officers and airmen continued to operate in what can only be described as separate class cultures. However, we can also see how the boundaries between these two groups were never fixed in any one-and-for-all sense. They changed and sometimes broke down, for example, during the pressures of war or even during foreign summer camps when a common sense of national identity overlaid class divisions.

Jim Steedman had completed his national service with the Royal Air Force and following his demob, he decided to join the AAF with a friend of his. He was offered the post of an Auxiliary Engineering Officer. He was responsible for supervising the servicing of aircraft such as the Vampire, on a daily basis. He was born in Billingham and was aware that Thornaby Aerodrome existed because he had visited it many times as a boy. In civilian life he was a draughtsman at ICI and he believed that the AAF was a good way to work with planes and to travel for summer camp. Many of his friends joined 608 Squadron with him, and he pointed out

"one of my friends came from Norton, he went to university, he was a metallurgist at ICI, we went to school together in Stockton, another came from Middlesbrough, he worked as an analyst for ICI, someone else came from County Durham, he worked for British Rail in a clerical job somewhere. Another chap, he came from Blyth, he worked for British Steel, and finally, one was a builder with his own business. We didn't enjoy our jobs so that's why we joined. Its not like joining a squadron in the Royal Air Force where you go and you don't know a soul, we nearly all were locals because how did you get to the Aerodrome, you had to be local."

Norman Winstanley having worked at Head Wrightsons at Thornaby, volunteered to join the regular RAF. He too was familiar with Thornaby Aerodrome because he had visited it as a boy. He was demobbed in 1946 and found the transition from service life to civilian life very difficult. He got a new job at ICI working in the laboratories, and although he enjoyed it, he saw an advert in the Evening Gazette which stated that 608 Squadron AAF were reforming at Thornaby. He went to the Aerodrome and volunteered to join as a pilot. He was immediately accepted and spent four years in the auxiliaries. He was a Warrant Officer pilot in the regular RAF, not an officer pilot, and when he joined 608 Squadron, he had to drop two ranks so he was actually a Sergeant pilot. That is interesting because prior to World War II, he would not have been accepted into the AAF as a pilot without a commission, and to obtain a commission he would have had to have a particular kind of background. Of his friends, one came from Middlesbrough and worked for Dorman Long, he was a navigator in the AAF, also a Warrant Officer, another man came from Ferry Hill, he was a Warrant Officer and he was an engineer both in civilian life and in the AAF. Another chap came from Ferry Hill as well and he worked as a linesman at the Electricity Board.

John Pollock, another ex 608 Squadron chap was born on 1st July 1922 in Thornaby, he worked as an apprentice range fitter at R W Crossthwaites which was associated with Thornaby Aerodrome because the airfield and the officers mess all belonged to Monty Crosthwaite. He joined the regular RAF as a wireless operator/air gunner. He was a Sergeant when he was demobbed and felt that he had met such wonderful chaps in the air force, and the RAF spirit was great and he wanted to be part of it again. He was in 608

Squadron right up until it was disbanded in 1957 and worked his way through the ranks to become a Squadron Leader, again an achievement that would not have been possible pre-war.

Alan Willis served in the RAF as a fighter pilot from 1942. He was born in Middlesbrough and he went to Acklam Hall School. When he came out of the RAF he worked at ICI. He joined 608 Squadron when it reformed in 1946 and maintained his rank and position as a pilot. He joined because he missed the comradeship and he missed flying. He was killed in an air crash flying a Vampire Jet back from 608 Squadron's Summer Camp in Malta on 12th September 1952.

Bob Harbron was born and brought up in Norton. He went to Westbury Street Primary School and then on to Arthur Head Senior School in Thornaby. His father was a long distance lorry driver. He left school at the age of fifteen and began work as an apprentice welder at a shipyard at Haverton Hill near Middlesbrough. He joined 608 Squadron in 1955 because it seemed like a challenge. He had other friends who were already members of the squadron. His trade was a trainee engine mechanic with a rank of AC2. In terms of skills, only the pilots had different skills to him, those working on the engineering side had the same skills as he did. He also said that officers would sit with the airmen if they were on a social evening, particularly when the squadron was on summer camp. When asked what kinds of positions the officers held in civilian life, he stated engineers, schoolteachers, dentists and businessmen. He volunteered to join the AAF rather than any other voluntary organisation because he was an ex air cadet, and he was aware that his employer approved of him being in the AAF, in fact he felt his employer readily encouraged him to volunteer. He joined 608 Squadron immediately upon leaving the RAF because quite simply he was missing the comradeship.

> "People talked the same language as you did, and they were all of the same character types. They had plumbers, fitters, and electricians. Quite honestly you could have called it the 608 ICI squadron. At least 80% of them you saw at ICI Billingham or at ICI Wilton. It was pride, pride in serving."

Another point that he made which related to both patriotism and voluntarism was

> "we had a pride in serving the country and in what we were

107

doing. What it is is the fact that if you have got pride and love of your country you are doing this and it is as simple as that. There is nothing gung ho about it or anything like that. I mean we were as much villains as you can think, well not villains, service men, but we enjoyed our selves and we never caused any problems or trouble. When we went to places like Germany or Malta or Gibraltar, we were ambassadors. We realised that. In fact being ambassadors of 608 Squadron or any of the auxiliary squadrons we were more sort of flying the flag, than the regular air force, because we were half way, we were civilian and military, and we realised that if we caused any trouble, it would not only act on the civilian side at home, it would act on the air force side. So therefore it was pride. It was a pride in the organisation."

In terms of socialising, again Mr Harbron used the Odd Fellows Public House and everyone would socialise together. On leaving 608 Squadron he went back to his old air training corps squadron and became a civilian instructor. He was also a Labour councillor and a Justice of the Peace.

Jim Steedman however noted that the officers still maintained a social distance because they:

> didn't have the squadron dances, but we used to go to an annual dance which was held in association with the Territorial Army and it was called the TAAFA Ball, that stood for Territorial Army and Air Force Association Ball, it was held at the Town Hall at Middlesbrough. I've got a photograph actually of us slightly worse the ware for drink, so yes we used to go to that one but we didn't have an individual squadron dance. We used to have cocktail parties and social weekends where wives would come up and join us on Saturday nights, but that was just for the officers and it was in the officers' mess.

Other activities of the officers caused consternation among local Stockton residents:

> in the Vane Arms there used to be a big brass, like one of those Eastern, I don't know what you would call it, not an urn but like one of them forty thieves jars, wider and made of brass, and they used to pinch it. It was on the stairs, halfway up, and they used to come back, one of the officers who had a car, and it would always be taken back, because the staff knew where it had gone. Then as

a punishment, they would put one of the lads inside it, and they would bash on the side of it, and it was called the brass band buggery box. The din was deafening if you were inside, it would make you go deaf.

Antics of this kind were reminiscent of the high-jinks that were common place in the officers' mess, but were seen as rather loutish and irresponsible by local residents.

Malcolm Ruecroft was born on 13th May 1934 in Trimdon Grange, County Durham. His father was a bricklayer. He went to school at Trimdon Grange County Mixed School and left at the age of fifteen. When he left school he became an apprentice painter and decorator. He joined 608 Squadron in 1952 at the age of eighteen. The reason he gave for joining the AAF was doing what I first wanted to do on leaving school. Wanting to become an RAF apprentice but my parents would not give me consent. He visited RAF Thornaby and joined 608 Squadron instead. Within the squadron he was a heavy goods driver and he also helped refuelling aircraft. He remembers that while in 608 Squadron he earned an annual bounty of one hundred pounds plus his service pay during the fifteen-day summer camp and weekend duties. Again he felt that the main differences that existed were found between the NCOs and the airmen. However, he was able to identify officers by their accents, which he termed "posh". He stated that the officers and the airmen would not socialise together, and that the airmen and NCOs frequented the Odd Fellows pub, 608 Squadron club and the NAAFI. When he left the AAF he became a fireman with the Durham County Fire Brigade.

Vic Fleming was born in Northern Ireland on 31st March 1938. He went to school in Lignacrieve Fintona. His father was a head teacher and his mother was a teacher. He left school at the age of fourteen and worked on a farm and in a grocers shop. He joined the RAF in 1936 because he had always wanted to be an airman. He was a technician and was promoted up to the rank of sergeant. He felt that there was no divide between the officers and the airmen and NCOs. In 1951 he joined 608 Squadron and he socialised with the other NCOs in the Odd Fellows Pub. He said that within the Squadron, all the ranks would sit together and that he was not aware of any differences between the ranks within that squadron. 608 Squadron was different to the regular RAF. It was much more of a family. A lot of my friends had already served in the RAF. On leaving 608

Squadron he became an engineer with The Commonwealth Aircraft Corporation of Australia. He also worked at ICI Wilton in the instrument section, and at the North Eastern Electricity Board as a shop manager.

George Crow was born on 14th June 1929 in Newcastle upon Tyne. He was brought up in East Rainton and this was where he went to school until he left at the age of fourteen. His father was a pavior and his mother did not work. When he left school he worked as an agricultural engineer. He joined 608 Squadron in 1950 and he was an armament mechanic holding the rank of Leading Aircraftsman. He was not aware of any divide between officers, NCOs and airmen although differences in uniforms were obvious. He used to socialise at the Odd Fellows Arms and would sometimes go into Stockton town centre. He remembers that generally the officers would socialise in the officer's mess. Several of his friends had been in the regular RAF. When he left the squadron he returned to his job as an agricultural engineer. Another man was a member of the regular RAF from 1941-1946. When he left the RAF he missed the comradeship that he had become used to and he decided to join 608 Squadron. He was an AC1, a flight mechanic air frames. He always socialised in the Odd Fellows arms. When asked how he got on with the officers and other ranks he said, fine, as an auxiliary, fine. It was totally different you see. They were all just blokes really. Well we were civilians so it wasn't the same as when we were in the RAF. When asked about socialising with the officers he stated you didn't mix closely very much, but if there was a social evening, a dance or something like that we were all there.

Ted Brown used to ride to Thornaby Aerodrome as a boy to watch the aircraft taking off and landing. He was called up for National Service in to the RAF, and on completion of this, he started work at ICI as an instrument basher. Whilst working at ICI, a friend of his, who was in 608 squadron as a sergeant, told him that 608 squadron was looking to recruit people. "In those days one never had a lot of money and the opportunity to go abroad, to work with aircraft, and to be paid by your company and to be paid by the RAF was something marvellous." He was interviewed by the CO, Squadron Leader Martin and he was told, "if you come in you have to do two weekends as an auxiliary and four nights." So he joined up in 1952 and travelled to Gibraltar, Malta, Germany and many other places, and he ended up doing three weekends and four nights. He was promoted up to corporal and then sergeant. He believed that there was not much contact between regular station staff and the auxiliary personnel stating, "as far as the section I was in, the regular would be around, not necessarily working. I suppose it was an opportunity for them to have time off really."

He also said that the officers kept to being officers and the men kept to being men.

"The only contact you had was flying. Most of the pilots were officers, but not every one. Most pilots were officers and it didn't matter whether you had brains or not, you would fly the aircraft. It wasn't the case as we progressed, the fittest and the brightest became pilots, but not before the war. They weren't the brightest by any means, and often it was, what was your family relationship, in what position you got really."

When asked about the reasons for joining the AAF again he talked about comradeship and money,

"most people who were in wanted to be in. They had volunteered for it. It wasn't a case of 'before I come in how much are you paying me?' I never questioned how much they were paying me. For me I could go back in and I could go abroad. I made friends, one lad was on airframes and he worked at ICI. Another man was the electrical sergeant and he became the works photographer at ICI Wilton, another chap was a sergeant and he worked at ICI."

Grant Goodwill, another pilot was born in Middlesbrough in 1932. He attended Hugh Bells School in Middlesbrough and his father was a test house manager at Head Wrightsons. He left school at fifteen and joined ICI in the research Department. He was called up for National Service in 1950 following growing speculation about the situation in Korea. After he had trained as a pilot during his time in the RAF, he went over to RAF Thornaby while he was on leave. He had the opportunity to sign up for another four years in the regular RAF but had been offered a Short Service Commission with 608 Squadron so he decided to leave the regulars and he joined 608 Squadron in 1953. He pointed out, when asked why he joined the AAF, they were very friendly and they did more flying than the regulars did.

"I could do my flying at weekends. Well it was a natural thing to do once I had come out of the RAF doing National Service. 608 Squadron were right on my doorstep and it was flying at weekends so I could carry on with my civvy job."

He of course stayed at the officer's mess at Thornaby and enjoyed being there so much that he nearly got the sack from British Type Press for taking too much time off. He used to go in during the week. During the day, Boss Martin would say "we have got some air firing on Thursday, are you coming in?" and I would just take the day off work.

When asked how much contact an officer would have with the airmen and NCOs he stated well if we met them in town we would say, "how do" and maybe have a drink with them, but we very rarely made arrangements with them. They kept themselves together and we kept ourselves together. On the airfield we came into contact with each other all the time. There were officers at 608 who weren't pilots, accounting officers, engineering officers and air traffic. The NCOs and the airmen were more on the engineering side of things, refuelling, checking tyres, aircraft maintenance and so on.

A normal weekend for a pilot at 608 was going on a Saturday morning.

"Occasionally you might go on a Friday night if you were going to go to RAF Ouston and form a wing. Then you would have what was known as a wingding for the weekend. You would form a wing; there would be 608 and 607 Squadron. We used to do that then there was a big exercise on with the RAF and join up with the regulars. But mainly we used to get there on a Saturday morning, maybe do a trip before lunch, and have lunch and then a trip in the afternoon. Finish by teatime and the same on a Sunday. But on a Sunday you started flying really early, and then sometimes we would have a spell of night flying, but that was usually on a weekday, a Thursday or Friday night."

He pointed out that the reality was

"it was just flying and keeping your hand in. I mean we were front line pilots. If a war had broken out, we would have gone straight into battle. One week we did battle formation at height practising cross over turns. Another week we would do rat and terrier, which was low-level interception. Then we would do air-to-air another weekend, and so it went on like that, just keeping your practice up. We used to do more flying than the regulars. More hours."

He noted that the

"Vampires weren't very big, they could do about 500 miles an hour at low level, they were very fast. If you swapped planes you would have to do a conversion on that. If you fly one aeroplane you can pilot another, it doesn't matter how big it is. You get the tuition and get some practise on it."

When asked why he volunteered for 608 Squadron and whether or not he was patriotic he said, "you went into the auxiliaries because you liked the flying. I was only twenty years old. It was great to take up an aircraft. Not many people did it. I mean there was no one around here who was in the flying game."

George Joyce was born in 1933 in Pelton Fell, near Chester Le Street, County Durham. His father was a durance bricklayer by trade and worked for Dorman Long in Middlesbrough. He was brought up in Middlesbrough and went to Hugh Bell School. He left school at fifteen and after he left school he went to work for ICI in the labs as a laboratory assistant. When he was called up to do his national service, one of his friends, who had already joined the RAF for his, suggested that he joined too. He was selected for pilot training and served within the RAF until 1953. He returned to the labs at ICI as an Analytical Laboratory Assistant (ALA) and when he found out that his friend had joined 608 Squadron, he immediately joined in 1953 and at that time, 608 Squadron were short of pilots. He served with the squadron from 1953 to 1957. Another of his friends who worked for British Rail also joined up on leaving the regular RAF, as did another chap who worked for a bank in Stockton and who had learned to fly in the regular RAF.

"It was interesting because we were sort of working five days a week and flying Saturdays and Sundays and Thursday nights. We were shattered, enjoying the socialising, the usual carry on, and after a few months of this, I had finished my six months course and qualified as an ALA, and the first shift they put me on was nights in this laboratory, and by eleven o'clock at night I couldn't keep my eyes open and I thought "oh I cant see me doing this for long, no way." And we were shattered anyway with flying all weekend and socialising, so the three of them all said "well something has got to give, I'll tell you what, we'll pack our jobs in." And so we became if you like, full time auxiliaries, which of course you weren't allowed to do. I think we did it for a while but after a year or two it got round, it got mentioned at Headquarters that there were three guys at Thornaby who were full time auxiliaries. So they brought a rule in that you could only do three days at a time, and then you had to have a day off, they used to cook the books and we used to get seven days one way or another, or six out of seven. We qualified for our flying pay, so for the best part of three years I was a regular auxiliary. It was just like a flying school, you had your own aircraft. Off you used to go."

In terms of the contact with the airmen he noted that

"the main contact we had with them was down on the flight. 608 Squadron had between twelve and sixteen planes and about twenty-two pilots. we used to fly our local area to keep our hand in. We were there as a reserve in the event of war breaking out. We were a reserve of trained pilots. There was a routine of exercises, up to high level, battle formation, gunnery against a towed target, air-to-air gunnery, low level battle formation, rat and terrier. Most people came in on a Thursday night and at weekends; we three were there all the time. We would do a couple of sorties on a Thursday night. Weekends you used to get quite a bit of flying, well we all used to average about thirty hours a month. That was a lot, much more than the regulars."

When the auxiliaries were disbanded in 1957, he became a commercial pilot until he retired.

David Stewart was with 608 Squadron between 1949 and 1952. He was a Warrant Officer Pilot who flew Spitfires and Vampires at Thornaby Aerodrome. He was born in Airdrie, 12 miles east of Glasgow, but was brought up in Canada from the age of four. Being mechanically inclined, and having witnessed the bombing in Plymouth he joined the Royal Air Force in 1943, and whilst posted to India, transferred to the Royal Canadian Air Force. In 1949, he was living in the North East of England, and missing the camaraderie and the flying, he joined 608 Squadron as a flight Sergeant in 1949, although he lived in Scarborough and travelled to Thornaby each day and at weekends by motorbike, a journey of one hour and twenty minutes each way. He was another regular auxiliary who used the AAF as a full time job. He noted "we had a good relationship as officers and NCOs because we were aircrew, and aircrew only. Also our lives depended on our ground crews. I did not socialise at all with other 608 personnel because I lived in Scarborough." On leaving 608 Squadron in 1952 he returned to Canada and joined 424 Squadron as a Flying Officer until 1957. He then worked in sales and management with Ford Motor Co dealers for thirty-five years.

These examples of officers and airmen who served in 608 Squadron after the Second World War highlight the fact that backgrounds were not important with regard to status within the Auxiliary Air Force. Recruitment for posts within the reforming 608 Squadron were not offered by word of mouth as they were before the war in the 1930s. Instead proper recruiting posters were placed around the local area, and also persistent notification of staff shortages were in local newspapers to try to raise the profile of the Squadron within the local vicinity. The evidence shows that the men who joined after the war tended to have already served within the regular RAF and that their decision to join the AAF was coloured by their love of planes, the comradeship that they missed, and also by their sense of duty to their country, patriotism. It was also based on their existing service careers and their experience rather than the position that their parents held within the local community. It is interesting to note that a great number of the men who were members of 608 Squadron worked for ICI. This supports the view that as an employer, ICI were very keen to be seen as fulfilling their role within the local community. By allowing their employees time off work to attend RAF Thornaby, they were seen to be playing an active part in the future of Teesside. This in turn raised their profile as a good, caring employer. Thus both the employer and the employee gained something positive from their involvement with the Auxiliary Air Force.

A Selection of Veterans Photographs

Mr John Pollock's Collection

Mr Honeyset's Collection

Mr Honeyset's Collection

Mr John Pollock's Collection

Mr John Pollock's Collection

Mr Honeyset's Collection

Mr Honeyset's Collection

Mr John Pollock's Collection

The End of it all

After the war and throughout the 1950s the auxiliary squadrons struggled to recruit sufficient numbers to maintain efficiency. Indeed, there had been concern about their efficiency since they had been reformed in 1946. In 1953 the top-secret "Baker-Carr Report", written by Air Commodore John Baker-Carr, stated that because of the limited amount of flying time that was available to an auxiliary pilot, future aeroplanes would be too complex for them to fly proficiently and the squadrons would therefore have had to be manned by ex-regulars. Furthermore, Baker-Carr believed that the auxiliary squadrons should all be disbanded. In 1954 the swept-wing supersonic fighter was created and the argument was put forward that since the nation was hard pressed to maintain its regular forces, the cost of new aircraft was so great that it would be cheaper to re-equip the fighter defence if there were less pilots.

Harold Macmillan as Defence Minister gained the nickname "Mac the Knife" in tribute to the sweeping defence cuts he proposed as a solution to Britain's economic malaise. He announced that it would not be possible, or indeed right, for auxiliaries to switch to the expensive new machines, a necessity if they were to remain in the front line of defence. He added that the government had decided to alter the organisation of this force to enable those Auxiliary pilots who could give their time to it to train on the swept-wing aircraft themselves as individuals; not to equip the squadrons with these machines, but to train the men. By this means they would provide reserves behind the regular squadrons in war. Thus, the role of the AAF was questioned and three areas were scrutinised.

Firstly, AAF fighter squadrons were called up for three months training in 1951 to prepare them for the Korean War. This upset many employers and the AAF were never called out again. Secondly, when NATO was created in 1949, the Air Ministry had declared all twenty auxiliary squadrons to be fully combat capable, but by 1953 they were no longer regarded as front-line units. Finally, people were increasingly giving way to advanced technology. By 1954 the Air Council and the Auxiliary and Reserve Forces Committee tried to find ways to sustain the flying squadrons; updating their aircraft was considered a possibility, as was reducing the number of squadrons from twenty to fifteen, however, aircraft technology was so advanced that it was not considered viable to give new aircraft to the AAF squadrons. By mid 1955 the Air Ministry was under increasing pressure to save money and the possibility was again discussed of disbanding the AAF squadrons.

By 1956, the Suez affair had strengthened the case for disbandment because of the drain on Britain's gold and dollar reserves. Some newspapers, and particularly those associated with Max Aitken, the former post-war Commanding Officer of 601 Squadron who ran the *Sunday Express,* began to leak details of total disbandment. No official comment came from the authorities resulting in protracted discussion in the press. However, in 1957 there was a major review of defence policy that culminated with a White Paper in 1957 from the Minister of Defence, Duncan Sandys'. This was announced in the aftermath of the Suez crisis and showed a major shift in defence policy by enforcing massive cuts in the number of troops and by increasing the dependence of the United Kingdom on nuclear technology. Furthermore, the disbandment of the AAF squadrons would save money immediately. It was decided - "the most effective deterrents for the United Kingdom were V Bombers and surface to air missiles."

The AAF leaders tried to fight the decision and formed a committee of the four metropolitan areas of London, composed of Squadron Leader, John Cormack of 600 Squadron who was an Esso executive, Tommy Turnbull of 604 Squadron who was a Lloyd's underwriter, Bob Eeles of 615 Squadron who was an ICI executive and Peter Edelston of 601, an advertising executive. The aim of the committee was to try to educate people in the role of the AAF in the hope that public opinion could stop the disbandment. They made a television appearance at the Pathfinders' Club in Knightsbridge and answered questions from the BBC air correspondent. They wrote to all Members of Parliament and all national and provincial newspapers. Their letter was therefore published all over

the country, highlighting their concern that the country is

throwing away an organisation whose worth is far greater than its face value, employing people whose time is spent productively five days a week and two days a week in the service of the crown. There is no doubt that the Royal Air Force is short of pilots, and disbanding the Auxiliary fighter squadrons means that the country will lose over 300 fully-trained fighter pilots, and in addition more than 2,000 ground crew.

They lobbied MPs and were always received with goodwill and sympathy, but effectively they were beaten. The decision was made and on 10th March 1957, the twenty Royal Auxiliary Air Force Squadrons were disbanded for the last time.

608 Squadron's final parade

LORD Swinton, Honorary Commodore, inspecting 608 (North Riding) Squadron, Royal Auxiliary Air Force, at the farewell parade held at RAF Station, Thornaby, yesterday. Later he took the salute at a march-past. The squadron will finally be disbanded on March 10.—[N.E.]

Former members of 608 Squadron came together for the last time in November 1959 at Middleton St George when The Standard, approved by the Queen, was presented by Air Vice-Marshall G H Ambler in the presence of Group Captain G Shaw, DFC, President of the Squadron Association, and other former officers and airmen. The Standard was later laid-up in York Minster.

After the war the airfield continued in use by the RAF as an air sea rescue base for Warwick aircraft and Sycamore Helicopters. The aerodrome became an air sea rescue station flying Sycamore helicopters. The rescuers developed the "Thornaby Bag" - a way in which food and first aid could be dropped to an aircrew that had been forced to abandon their aircraft. In October 1958 the airfield closed to flying and was vacated by the RAF.

For a short time the site was used as a motor racing circuit with the names of Hudson straight, Anson straight, Hawker hairpin, Hurricane corner, Gladiator bends, and defiant corner. The modern town of Thornaby was built on the site of the redundant aerodrome with many of the road names having an aviation connection. Mitchell Avenue is named after RJ Mitchell, who designed the Spitfire, while Trenchard Avenue honours Lord Trenchard the founding father of the Royal Air Force. Flying ceased on 1st. Oct. 1958 and the airfield was sold to the council on 23rd February 1962 as the site of the new Thornaby Town Centre. In October 2005, the aircraft hanger, one of the last links to the aerodrome was demolished.

No. 608 (NORTH RIDING) SQUADRON

ROYAL AUXILIARY AIR FORCE

Consecration and Presentation of the

Squadron Standard

Royal Air Force   Sunday, 1st November, 1959

Middleton St. George   at 3 p.m.

124

CONSECRATION OF THE STANDARD

Here follows the Consecration of the Standard

The Senior Officer : Reverend Sir, on behalf of No. 608 Squadron we ask you to bid God's blessing on this Standard.

Chaplain : We are ready to do so.

We are gathered here to consecrate this Standard, the solemn symbol of our loyalty, and with it ourselves, our service, and our life. May this Standard never be unfurled save in the cause of justice, righteousness and truth.

Let us pray. (Spectators should stand).

Chaplain : Our help is in the name of the Lord.

All : Who hath made heaven and earth.

Chaplain : The Lord be with you.

All And with thy spirit.

Chaplain : To the Glory of God and as a symbol of our duty to Him and of our service to our Sovereign Lady Queen Elizabeth, we consecrate this Standard in the name of the Father, and of the Son, and of the Holy Ghost.

All Amen.

Chaplain : Let us Pray.

All : Our Father, which art in heaven, hallowed be Thy Name, Thy Kingdom come, Thy will be done on earth as it is in heaven ; Give us this day our daily bread and forgive us our trespasses, as we forgive them that trespass against us ; and lead us not into temptation, but deliver us from evil ; for Thine is the kingdom, the power and the glory, for ever and ever : Amen.

Chaplain : O God, the Protector of all that trust in Thee, without Whom nothing is strong, nothing is holy ; Increase and multiply upon us Thy mercy, that, Thou being our Ruler and Guide, we may so pass through things temporal, that we finally lose not the things eternal : Grant this, O Heavenly Father, for Jesus Christ's sake, our Lord, Amen.

GOD SAVE THE QUEEN.

All : Amen.

Chaplain : God be with you.

All : Amen.

608 (N.R.) SQUADRON ASSOCIATION.

The President & Mrs. G. Shaw and members of the Association

request the pleasure of the company of

Mr. J. Pollock & Guest.

at Royal Air Force, Middleton St. George, on Sunday, 1st November, 1959, at 3 p.m., when The Standard of No. 608 (N.R.) Squadron, Royal Auxiliary Air Force, will be presented to the Association by Air Vice Marshal G. H. Ambler, C.B., C.B.E., A.F.C., and also at York on Saturday, 14th November, 1959, at 4 p.m. for the Laying-Up Ceremony in the Minster.

Reception at Middleton.
Plain Clothes—Decorations.

R.S.V.P. 24th October :
P. VARTY, Hon. Secretary,
High Leven, Yarm

A Selection of Veterans Photographs

Mr Ron Lawson's Collection

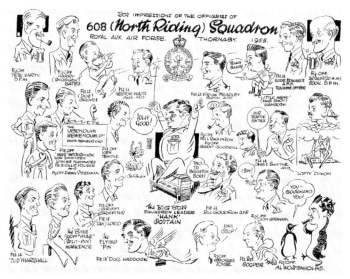

Mr John Pollock's Collection

Left to right
Neil Hancock, Mac McKenzie, George Joyce, Bill Goodrum, Hank Costain,
Bill Swainston, Judd Marshall, Harry Bates, Cooper and ?

Mr John Pollock's Collection

Left to Right
George Martin (CO), George Joyce, Neil Hancock and Mac McKenzie

Mr John Pollock's Collection

Left to Right
  Harry Bates, George Joyce, ?, Mac McKenzie, Neil Hancock, ?, ?, Vic Fleming and Hank Costain

Mr John Pollock's Collection

John Pollock and Jack Thurston
Mr John Pollock's Collection

Mr John Pollock's Collection

Mr John Pollock's Collection

Mr John Pollock's Collection

Mr John Pollock's Collection

Mr John Pollock's Collection

Mr John Pollock's Collection

George Davies Collection

Mr John Pollock's Collection

Mr John Pollock's Collection

Mr John Pollock's Collection

Former Commanding Officers of 608 Squadron
Left to Right
George Martin, ?, Hank Costain, Geoffrey Ambler, William Appleby-Brown
Mr John Pollock's Collection

Bill Sykens in a Spitfire
Mr John Pollock's Collection

Princess Margaret visiting Squadron Leader Robinson and 608 Squadron
Mr John Pollock's Collection

Farewell Ball 1957
Mr John Pollock's Collection

Remembering Thornaby Aerodrome and 608 Squadron Royal Auxiliary Air Force

The Memorial

In September 1996, Thornaby Town Council formed a committee to consider the possibility of putting a memorial on the site of the old aerodrome. Many RAF veterans, aircraft enthusiasts and local businesses teamed up to launch a fund raising appeal with a target of £10,000. Vaux Breweries donated £250 to the appeal in memory of Flight Commander Peter Vaux, a relative of the brewing family, who had served with 608 Squadron.

Flight Lieutenant John Pollock, a veteran from 608 Squadron, took on the role of campaign organiser, and noted "the aerodrome closed in 1948, but residents, both military and civilian, served or worked there and still recall the important role it played in their lives.

The memorial was designed by Mr David Shuttleworth from Eaglescliffe, a retired architect and former Lancaster bomber navigator. The bronze figure was made by Mr Tony Maw in his Green Dragon Yard studio in Stockton. Whilst the Yorkshire sandstone plinth was hand-carved by Mr Bob Weatherill from Danby. There is an important connection between Thornaby Aerodrome and Danby – a radar station on Danby Beacon was parented and supported by RAF Thornaby throughout the war.

The statue, standing on a stone plinth is meant to symbolise all who have served at Thornaby Aerodrome during its years of operational service.

The memorial was dedicated in a service on 8th May 1997. This was attended by civic dignitaries, over 200 service veterans and their families and local clergy. Wing Commander Hank Costain, who was the last Commanding Officer of 608 Squadron performed the ceremony and the memorial was blessed by Squadron Leader Kevin Maddy, the padre from RAF Leeming.

Thornaby Gateway – Spitfire Project

In 2002, a decision was taken by Thornaby Town Council and Stockton Borough Council to apply to the Heritage Lottery Fund for a grant of £50,000 to place a replica spitfire on a key gateway into Thornaby alongside an extensive educational programme. The idea was to celebrate Thornaby's past and in particular, the role of the Aerodrome in World War Two.

As the scheme became public there was much local debate about the decision to select a spitfire as the replica aircraft. Many local enthusiasts were outraged at the selection arguing that the Lockheed Hudson had been the most significant aircraft to be flown at Thornaby during World War Two, but initial costing of a replica Hudson suggested £450,000, which clearly was out of reach of the project.

In March 2006 I was appointed as the project historian. My job was to research and write the three interpretation panels which would be located on the Thornaby Road and Bader Avenue roundabout. The first panel was entitled RAF Thornaby on Tees 1912-1939, The second panel, RAF Thornaby on Tees 1939-1945, and the final panel was RAF Thornaby on Tees 1946-1958. I was also asked to write an education pack for teachers across the Borough which focussed on the development of aircraft types through the years.

My initial research took me back to the National Archives at Kew in London to establish that the choice of replica aircraft, a Spitfire Vb, was authentic to Thornaby Aerodrome. My research showed that one section of 403 Squadron Royal Canadian Air Force was based at Thornaby, on detachment from Catterick, flying Spitfire Vb's in January 1944. They were then replaced by No 401 Squadron RCAF and finally No 306 Polish Squadron arrived on 29th May remaining at Thornaby until 11th August 1944.

Once the aircraft authenticity was established, plans went ahead to have the aircraft made. Although letters to the local press reflected the split in local public opinion as to the choice of aircraft, the committee were happy with the decision.

On Thursday March 8th 2007 the Spitfire was lowered into place with crowds gathering to watch a huge crane lift the plane into place on Thornaby Road which is a gateway into the town. The letters on the side of the Spitfire are the code letters of the two squadrons which flew Spitfires from RAF Thornaby.

The dedication ceremony took place on Sunday 1st April 2007, attended by members of Thornaby Town Council, representatives from RAF Leeming, RAF veterans and other dignitaries.

Conclusion

Having spent the last seven years researching the English squadrons of the Auxiliary Air Force, and a similar amount of time studying 608 Squadron and Thornaby Aerodrome, I am happy to have written this book detailing their combined histories, and the memories of many of the veteran's and their families whom I have interviewed.

I feel privileged to have played even a small role in ensuring that the history of both the Squadron and the Aerodrome remain uppermost in the minds of local people, and particularly, in the minds of the younger generation whose job it is to carry their histories into the future.

Over the last ten years, local residents of Thornaby, as well as Thornaby Town Council and to a certain extent, Stockton on Tees Borough Council have worked hard to erect both the memorial and the Spitfire, and have channelled money into the Teacher's Pack which I have written to assist in the education of local primary school pupils.

There are few remaining veterans from 608 Squadron, and it is very sad to think that within the next decade or so, there will be no one left who served at the Aerodrome. It is our duty to ensure that their memories live on, and that Thornaby's history is recognised and celebrated.

APPENDIX 1

Squadrons serving at RAF Thornaby on Tees 1930 –1957

Year	Squadron No	Left Thornaby	Aircraft
1930	608 (NR) Auxiliary Air Force	December 1941	Avro 504N Lynx Trainer
			Westland Wapiti
			Hawker Demon
			Avro Anson
			Bristol Blenheim
			Blackburn Botha
			Lockheed Hudson
1937	9 Flying Training School	April 1937	Hawker Hart Trainers
		September 1938	Avro Anson
	233 (General Reconnaissance)		
	224(General Reconnaissance)	September 1938	Lockheed Hudson
1938	106	August 1939	Fairey Battle
	185	August 1939	Fairey Battle
	220	April 1941	Avro Anson
			Lockheed Hudson
	269 (General Reconnaissance)	October 1938	Avro Anson
	42 Squadron	October 1938	Vickers Vildebeest
1940	224 (General Reconnaissance)	June 1940	Lockheed Hudson
1941	114 (Hong Kong)	May 1941	Bristol Blenheim
	143	October 1941	Bristol Beaufighter F Mk 1c
	6 (C) Operational Training Unit	March 1943	Lockheed Hudson
	1429 (Czechoslovakian) Flight	October 1943	Wellington
1943	403 (Royal Canadian Air Force)	January 1943	Spitfire Vb
	401 (Royal Canadian Air Force)	May 1943	Spitfire Vb
	306 (Polish)	August 1943	Spitfire Vb
	280 Air Sea Rescue	May 1944	Avro Anson
			Vickers Warwick
	281 Air Sea Rescue	February 1944	Vickers Warwick
	1 (C) Operational Training Unit	October 1943	Lockheed Hudson
1944	279 Air Sea Rescue	September 1945	Lockheed Hudson
			Vickers Warwick
1945	455 Squadron Royal Australian Air Force	May 1945	Bristol Beaufighter
1946	608 (NR) Auxiliary Air Force	March 1957	Mosquito N F 30
			Oxford T2
			Spitfire F22
			De Haviland Vampire F3
			Meteor T7
			Harvard T26
			De Haviland Vampire FB5
			De Haviland Vampire FB9
1954	275 Squadron Air Sea Rescue	November 1954	Sycamore Helicopter

APPENDIX 2

The following appendix lists the officers of 608 Squadron Auxiliary Air Force. The date of commission has been obtained by using www.gazette-online.co.uk and searching the archive for 608 squadron personnel. Date of commission data is found in the Supplements to the London Gazette for the date given.

Where material has been found from press records, interviews, books or the internet, this has been indicated. This appendix forms part of a much wider piece of research on all of the English Auxiliary Air Force squadrons.

608 (North Riding) Squadron

Charles Edward John Dingle   07/09/1937

Alan Strafford Johnson   17/02/1936

Son of Mr S J Johnson and Mrs Johnson of Birkdale. Marriage announcement in Times.

John Buchanon Gibson   01/11/1937

Stanley Whittaker Jackson   19/06/1935

Geoffrey Hill Ambler   07/02/1931

Marriage announcement in Times. Son of Mr Fred Ambler and Mrs Ambler of Chellow Grange, Bradford, Yorkshire. Grandson of Sir James Hill, who was the owner of James Hill & Sons Ltd, the largest private wool merchants in the country, and also Liberal MP for Bradford Central. Geoffrey's father, Frederick Ambler, owned Midland Mills in Bradford, his mother, Annie Hill, was the sister of Sir James Hill. Geoffrey was born at Baildon in 1904 and was educated at Shrewsbury and rowed for the school at Henley in 1922. He attended Clare College, Cambridge where he obtained his BA degree and rowed in the winning university crews of 1924, 1925 and 1926. By 1930 he was Director of Fred Ambler Limited of Bradford, his fathers woollen firm. A member of Yorkshire Aeroplane Club, he already had his pilots license and owned his own plane.

143

Wilfred Urwin Hodson   23/12/1930

John Lionel Clayton   07/02/1931

Harry Clayton's family owned a well-known retail business in Middlesbrough

Ivo Wilfred Home Thompson   29/08/1930

Son of Sir Wilfrid and Lady Thompson of Old Nunthorpe.

Ralph Arden Clay   20/10/1934

Geoffrey Whitley Garnett   14/11/1936

Philip Kay Stead   19/04/1937

Marriage announcement in Times. Lived at Hillside, Glenhow, Leeds.

Cosmo William Wright   21/07/1931

Marriage announcement in Times. Comes from West Lawn, Sunderland. Family were clothiers in the Tower House in Middlesbrough.

Peter Douglas Ord Vaux   20/07/1933

Marriage announcement in Times. Younger son of Colonel Ernest Vaux CMG and DSO, Brettanby Manor, Barton, Yorkshire. Also wedding announcement in Times. Court circular announcement 1980 in Times announces service of thanksgiving for life of Wing Commander Peter Douglas Ord Vaux at St Cuthbert and St Mary Church, Richmond. Born in Grindon near Sunderland. He went to school at Harrow and then went on to Cambridge University where he joined the University Air Squadron and learned to fly. He was commissioned into the Auxiliary Air Force in July 1933 and he lived at Piercebridge in County Durham. He was an amateur jockey who rode in the Grand National and took part in various point to points. He rode with the Zetland and Bedale Hunts. He was also connected to the brewing side of the family.

Anthony Neville Wilson   10/02/1931

Family were clothiers in the Tower House in Middlesbrough.

James William Woolcock   06/05/1937

Henry Charles Newhouse   05/01/1933

Came from one of the villages outside Middlesbrough, he attended Cambridge University and his family owned Newhouses Department Store in Middlesbrough.

William Appleby Brown   07/02/1938

From Saltburn, his father was James Brown, who worked for the family firm J Brown and Co who were builder's merchants at Queens Square in Middlesbrough. The Brown family was a prominent Middlesbrough family that included Alderman John Wesley Brown who was MP for Middlesbrough in 1921. His family also had a shipping company called Lion Shipping that imported iron ore from Spain and Timber from the Baltic States.

Hugh Jenkin Williams   19/06/1935

Henry Peter Graham Gray   07/02/1938

Michael John Cecil Hutton-Wilson   27/02/1932

Geoffrey Shaw   29/08/1930

Came from Nunthorpe and his family owned W G Shaw Engineering Co in North Ormesby. His father W G Shaw was the President of the Middlesbrough branch of the Institute of British Foundry men. Geoffrey was educated in Scotland but then attended Cambridge University where he learned to fly as part of the University Air Squadron. He also owned his own aeroplane that he used for long business trips. He took part in the MacRobertson Air Race from England to Australia in 1934.

William Howard Davis   28/04/1930

Son of RW and JP Howard Davis of Elton House, Darlington. He lived in Saltburn. He worked as Chief Accountant to Dorman Long.

Keith Pyman   07/02/1938

Member of Hurworth Hunt. Marriage announcement in Times. Son of Frederick H Pyman JP and Mrs Pyman, Dunsley Hall, Sandsend near Whitby. He lived at Far End, Yarm.

Robert Burrell   15/12/1938

Marriage announcement in Times. Son of Mr R Burrell and Mrs L Burrell of Glenwyne, Scorrier, Cornwall.

John Glynn Considine   15/12/1938

Jerome Francis Lambert   15/12/1938

Dennis Baird   11/09/1937

Came from West Hartlepool, family business, J W Baird and Company Ltd was importing various kinds of wood.

Philip Lloyd-Graeme   16/12/1934

Sir Philip Cunliffe Lister, a member of the Lloyd-Graeme family from Sewerby Hall and estate in the East Riding of Yorkshire. His father in law was Sir John Cunliffe-Lister, Baron of Masham and chief shareholder in Manningham Mills. Philip was educated at Winchester and University College Oxford. He was a barrister and a Conservative MP and he served in the squadron before the war, returning as Honorary Air Commodore under the name of the Rt Hon Viscount Swinton.

John Sherburn Priestly (Pip) Phillips   04/01/1937

Born in Dublin in November 1919; his father John Skelton Phillips was in the army whilst his mother was related to J B Priestly. He attended St Olave's School in York before moving to the senior school, St Peter's School in York on 23rd January 1933 where he was a full boarder. He left the school in July 1936 and moved to Crooksbarn Lane in Norton; Stockton on Tees. He was a successful rower for the school and he was a cadet in the OTC. He worked as an engineer in Darlington, employed by the London North Eastern Railway, joining 608 Squadron in 1937 at the age of 18.

P Kennedy   14/08/1938

Came from Middlesbrough and had attended Oxford University. He was an accountant at ICI.

APPENDIX 3

Ground plan of Thornaby Aerodrome[1]

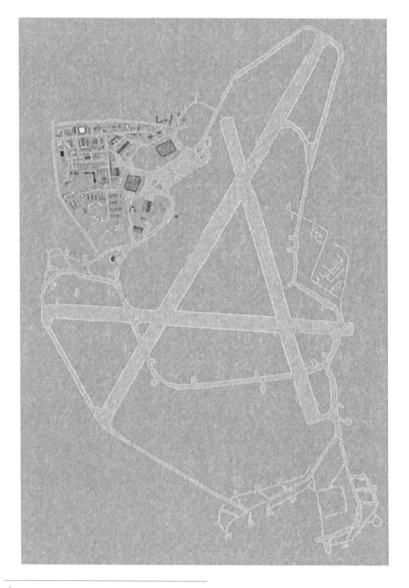

---

[1] http://hammer.prohosting.com/~thornaby/

APPENDIX 4

Ground Plan of Buildings at Thornaby Aerodrome

[2] http://hammer.prohosting.com/~thornaby/

149

APPENDIX 5

The Indomitable spirit of wartime Britain showed clearly in the larrikin and lighthearted behaviour so often adopted by the soldiers, sailors and airmen who flirted with death for King and Country. How many Teessiders remember this favourite from Thornaby Air Force Station?

Delaney's Donkey

Now you've heard Delaney's donkey, how it won the half mile race,

But if you want some real good laughs, the Air Force is the place,

And the day that I remember best in all my memories

Was the day they dished the rifles out at Thornaby-on-Tees

They were pushing them, poling them, showing them and choking them

Young Bill Todd was knocking at the knees

They were dragging them, swinging them, carrying them and slinging them

The day they dished the rifles out at Thornaby-on Tees

Some held their guns like shovels, with barrels on the ground

While some were climbing up 'em to have a look around.

When Martin swung his rifle as though it were a spear,

It took three men to pull it out of Curly Warden's ear.

So they got the airmen ready and they stood 'em in a row

They took the rifles off us 'cos we couldn't make 'em go

Then they went along the line, gave us pea shooters and peas

The day they passed the rifles out at Thornaby-on-Tees.

BIBLIOGRAPHY

Primary Sources

Interviews

Mr P Alexander, Birmingham, Saturday 6th August 2005.
Mrs E Appleby-Brown, Saltburn by Sea, Saturday 16th March 2002.
Mrs. V. Bracknell, Guisborough, Sunday 12th March 2006.
Mr Ted Brown, Boosebeck, Wednesday 12th November 2003.
Mr Sydney Buckle, Stockton on Tees. Saturday 15th November 2003.
Mr Harold Coppick, Billingham, Monday 20th October 2003.
Mr G. Crow, Belmont, Saturday 27th March 2004.
Mr Walter Hilary Davies, Great Ayton, Tuesday 23rd November 2004.
Mr. Vic. Fleming, Redcar, Tuesday 18th November 2003.
Mrs. J. Gilbert, Stockton on Tees, Friday 19th April 2002.
Mr Grant Goodwill, Middlesbrough, Thursday 11th November 2004.
Mr. Albert Guy, Newton Aycliffe, Saturday 6th March 2004
Mr T. Harbron, Stockton on Tees, Tuesday 11th November 2003.
Mr. S.J. Hawksfield, Billingham, Friday 9th May 2003.
Mr A. Huitson, Stockton on Tees, Thursday 13th November 2003.
Mrs Valerie Kayll, Witton Gilbert, Durham, Monday 25th July 2005.
Mr G. Joyce, Billingham, Friday 12th November 2004.
Mr. D. Lambert, Abingdon, Saturday 25th October 2003.
Mr. D. Landing, Stockton on Tees, Tuesday 5 July 2005.
Mr C. Matthews, Chilton Moor, Thursday 22nd November 2001.
Mr. P. Meston, Bearsden, Glasgow, Thursday 6th January 2005.
Mr G. Milburn, Ilderton, Friday 21st November 2003.
Mr John Pollock, Stockton on Tees, Monday 3rd December 2001.
Mr M. Ruecroft, Trimdon Grange, Friday 2nd April 2004.
Mr. C. Quinn, Middlesbrough, Tuesday 21st March 2006.
Mr Jim Steedman, Stockton on Tees, Saturday 18th October 2003.
David Stewart, Friday 19th March 2004. Internet interview
Wing Commander Ken Stoddart, Monday 25th July 2005.
Mrs. V. Sykes, Middlesbrough, Saturday 1st November 2003.
Mrs. H. Thrower, Stockton on Tees, Monday 7th January 2002.
Mr Peter Vaux's son, Darlington, Friday 18th November 2005.
Mr Ronnie Waterson, Billingham, Monday 15th November 2004.
Mr George Williams, Sunningdale, Ascot, Monday 3rd January 2005.
Mrs. A. Willis, Eaglescliffe, Thursday 4th November 2004.
Mr N. Winstanley, Stockton on Tees, Thursday 30th October 2003.
Mr. C. Wright, Monday 13th December 2004.

Newspapers

Daily Telegraph,1937.
Eastern Weekly News,1948.
The Gazette, 1937 – 1941.
The Guardian Digital Archive 1821-2000
The London Gazette, 1926 – 1957.
North Eastern Daily Gazette, 1930 – 1958.
North Eastern Weekly News, 1947.
Northern Daily Mail, 1947.
Northern Echo, 1946 - 1947.
The Times Digital Archives, 1925 – 1985.
Yorkshire Post, 1946.

National Archives

Air 2/338. Purchase of Land at Thornaby-on-Tees from Trustees of R.W. Crosthwaite (deceased) 1928 - 1930.

Air 2/263. Air Ministry and Successors: Operational Record Book, 608 (North Riding) Squadron Auxiliary Air Force 1930 - 1957.

Air 15/146. Re-equipment of 500 and 608 Squadrons with Aircraft Rocket Weapons: Report May – July 1943.

Air 27/2097. 608 Squadron: Operations Record Book March 1930 – December 1940.

Air 27/2676. 608 Squadron January 1951 – December 1954.

Air 27/2712. 608 Squadron February 1955 – March 1957.

Air 27. Air Ministry and Successors: Operational Record Book, RAF Thornaby Station 1930 – 1957.

Air 28/824. Operational Record Book, RAF Thornaby June 1937 – December 1941.

Air 28/825. Operational Record Book, RAF Thornaby February 1942 – December 1943.

Air 28/826. Operational Record Book, RAF Thornaby January 1944 – December 1945.

Air 28/827. Operational Record Book, RAF Thornaby October 1939 – January 1940.

Air 28/828. Operational Record Book, RAF Thornaby September 1939 – October 1943.

Air 28/829. Operational Record Book, RAF Thornaby February 1940 – May 1940

Air 28/830. Operational Record Book, RAF Thornaby June 1940 – August 1940.

Air 28/824. Operational Record Book, RAF Thornaby June 1937 – December 1941.

Air 28/831. Operational Record Book, RAF Thornaby September 1940 – December 1940.

Air 28/832. Operational Record Book, RAF Thornaby January 1941 – March 1941.

Air 28/833. Operational Record Book, RAF Thornaby April 1941 – June 1941.

Air 28/834. Operational Record Book, RAF Thornaby July 1941 – December 1941.

Air 28/835. Operational Record Book, RAF Thornaby January 1942 – December 1942.

Air 28/836. Operational Record Book, RAF Thornaby January 1942 – December 1944.

Air 28/837. Operational Record Book, RAF Thornaby January 1945 – December 1945

Air 28/1132. Operational Record Book, RAF Thornaby January 1946 – June 1946 and July 1950 – December 1950.

Air 28/1276. Operational Record Book, RAF Thornaby January 1951 – December 1955.

Air 28/1428. Operational Record Book, RAF Thornaby January 1956 – October 1958.

Air 49/275. 608 Squadron RAF: Reports May 1943 – June 1944.

Other Primary Sources

608 Squadron Scrapbook in possession of Mrs. E. Appleby-Brown.
Teesside Archives File No. 125, Thornaby Aerodrome.
Teesside Archives File No U/Bar – J W Baird and Company Ltd
Avril Pedley, Archivist and Alumni Officer, St Peter's School, Clifton, York, YO30 6AB.

Birch, A.H.	*Small Town Politics – A Study of Political Life in Glossop* (London, 1959).
Bishop, Patrick	*Fighter Boys Saving Britain 1940* (London, 2004).
Black, Jeremy	*Maps and History – Constructing Images of the Past* (London, 1997).
Blunt, Barry	*608 Mosquito Bomber Squadron* (Stockport, 1998).
Bond, Brian	*British Military Policy Between the Two World Wars* (Oxford, 1980).
Borsay, Peter	*A History of Leisure* (Basingstoke, 2006).
Bourne, J M	*Britain and the Great War 1914 – 1918* (New York, 1989).
Bowyer, Chaz	*The History of the RAF* (London, 1977).
Bowyer, Chaz	*The Royal Air Force 1939 – 1945* (Barnsley, 1996).
Bowyer, Michael J F	*Aircraft for the Few. The RAF's Fighters and Bombers in 1940* (Yeovil Somerset, 1991).
Boyle, Andrew	*Trenchard* (London, 1962).
Branson, Noreen &	*The History of British Society.*
Heinemann, Margaret	*Britain in the Nineteen Thirties* (London, 1971).
Brooks, Robin J.	*Kent's Own. The History of 500 (County of Kent) Squadron Royal Auxiliary Air Force* (Gillingham Kent, 1982).
Brown, David	*Thornaby Aerodrome and Wartime Memories* (Stockton, 1992).

Brown, David — Bombs by the Hundred on Stockton on Tees (Stockton, 1990).

Brown, E. — Wings on My Sleeve (London, 2006).

Burns, M.G. — Bader, the Man and his Men (London, 1990).

Bush, M L — Social Orders and Social Classes. Europe Since 1500 (Harlow, 1992).

Butler, Tim & Savage, Mike (eds), — Social Change and the Middle Classes (London, 1995).

Calder, Angus — The Myth of the Blitz (London, 1992).

Cannadine, David — Aspects of Aristocracy. Grandeur and Decline I n Modern Britain, (New Haven, 1994).

Cannadine, David — Class in Britain (London, 1998).

Cannadine, David — The Decline and Fall of the British Aristocracy (New Haven, 1990).

Cannadine, David — Lords and Landlords: The Aristocracy and the Towns 1774 – 1967 (Leicester, 1980).

Carr, E.H. — What is History (London, 1990).

Catterall, Peter — British History 1945 – 1987: An Annotated Biography (Oxford, 1990).

Caunce, Stephen — Oral History and the Local Historian (London, 1994).

Chamier, J.A. — The Birth of the Royal Air Force (London, 1943).

Chorlton, Martyn — Airfields of North-East England in the Second World War (Newbury, 2005).

Chun, Lin — The British New Left (Edinburgh, 1993).

Clark, Alan — Aces High. The War in the Air over the Western Front 1914 – 1918 (London, 1973).

Clarke, Graham — The Photograph (Oxford, 1997).

Clayton, P.B. (MC, FSA) — Tales of Talbot House: Everyman's Club in Poperinghe & Ypres 1915-1918 (London, 1919).

Clayton, T. & Craig, P.   *Finest Hour* (London, 1999).

Coombs, L.F.E.   *The Lion has Wings. The Race to Prepare the RAF for World War II: 1935 - 1940* (Shrewsbury, 1997).

Crockett, Richard   *Twilight of Truth. Chamberlain, Appeasement and the Manipulation of the Press* (London, 1989).

Crompton, Rosemary   *Class and Stratification. An Introduction to Current Debates* (Cambridge, 1998).

Cronin, James E.   *The Politics of State Expansion – War, State and Society in Twentieth Century Britain* (London, 1991).

Cross, J.A.   *Lord Swinton* (Oxford, 1982).

Crossick, Geoffrey (ed)   *The Lower Middle Class in Britain 1870 – 1914* (London, 1977).

Cunningham, Hugh   *The Volunteer Force: A Social and Political History 1895 -1908* (London, 1975).

Davidson, M. & Taylor J.   *Spitfire Ace. Flying the Battle of Britain* (London, 1988).

Dean, Sir Maurice   *The Royal Air Force and Two World Wars* (London, 1979).

De Groot, Gerard J.   *"Blighty. British Society in the Era of the Great War"* (Harlow Essex,1996).

De Groot, Gerard J.   *The First World War* (Basingstoke, 2001).

Deighton, L.   *Fighter. The True Story of the Battle of Britain* (London, 1977).

Delve, Ken & Pitchfork, Graham   *South Yorkshire's Own. The Story of 616 Squadron* (Exeter, 1990).

Dennis, Peter   *The Territorial Army 1906-1940* (Suffolk, 1987).

Des Honey, J.R.   *Tom Brown's Universe. The Development of the Victorian Public School* (London, 1977).

Dickson, Wing Commander Alex (ed)   *The Royal Air Force Volunteer Reserve – Memories* (RAF Innsworth Gloucester, 1997).

Donnison, David & Soto, Paul — The Good City – A Study of Urban Development and Policy in Britain (London, 1980).

Dundas, H. — Flying Start. A Fighter Pilots War Years (London, 1988).

Elias, Norbert — The Civilizing Process (Oxford, 1994).

Evening Gazette, — Teesside at War – A Pictorial Account 1939 – 1945 (Manchester, 1989).

Ferguson, Aldon P. — Beware Beware! The History of 611 (West Lancashire) Squadron Royal Auxiliary Air Force (Reading, 2004).

Finlayson, Geoffrey — Citizen, State and Social Welfare in Britain 1830 – 1990 (Oxford, 1994).

Fisher, Nigel — Harold MacMillan. A Biography (London, 1982).

Floud, J.E.(ed), Halsey, A.H., Martin, F.M. — Social Class and Educational Opportunity (London,1956).

Fredette, Raymond H. — The First Battle of Britain 1917/1918 and the Birth of the Royal Air Force (London, 1966).

Fuchser, Larry William — Neville Chamberlain and Appeasement. A Study in the Politics of History (London, 1982)

Gathorne-Hardy, Jonathan — The Public School Phenomenon (Sevenoaks Kent, 1977).

Giddens, Anthony — Classes, Power and Conflict (London, 1981).

Giddens, Anthony — The Class Structure of the Advanced Society (London, 1973).

Goldthorpe, John H. — Social Mobility and Class Structure in Modern Britain (Oxford, 1987).

Goodson, James — Tumult in the Clouds. The Classic Story of War in the Air (London, 2003).

Grant, R.G. — Flight. 100 Years of Aviation (London, 2004).

Grayson, Richard S. — Austen Chamberlain and the Commitment to Europe. British Foreign Policy 1924 – 1929 (London, 1997).

Gunn, Simon   *History and Cultural Theory* (Harlow, 2006).

Gunn, Simon &
Rachel Bell   *Middle Classes: Their Rise and Sprawl* (London, 1988)

Gunn, Simon   *The Public Culture of the Victorian Middle Class. Ritual and Authority in the English Industrial City 1840 – 1914* (Manchester, 2000). Hall, Jeffrey *Sport, Leisure and Culture in Twentieth Century Britain* (London, 2002).

Halpenny, Bruce Barrymore   *Action Stations: 4, Military Airfields of Yorkshire* Cambridge, 1982).

Halsey, A.H.   *Change in British Society from 1900 to the Present Day* (Oxford, 1995).

Halsey, A.H.(ed) with
Webb, Josephine   *Twentieth Century British Social Trends* (Basingstoke, 2000).

Hannah, Leslie   *The Rise of the Corporate Economy* (London, 1976).

Harley, J.B.   *Maps for the Local Historian – A Guide to the British Sources* (London, 1972).

Harris, Paul P.   *This Rotarian Age* (Chicago, 1935).

Hering, Sqn. Ldr. P.G.   *Customs and Traditions of the Royal Air Force* (Aldershot, 1961).

Heywood, Andrew   *Political Ideologies. An Introduction* (Basingstoke, 1998).

Hill, Jeffrey   *Sport, Leisure and Culture in Twentieth Century Britain* (Basingstoke, 2002).

Hindle, Brian Paul   *Maps for Local History* (London, 1988).

Hinton, James   *Women, Social Leadership and the Second World War. Continuities of Class* (Oxford, 2002).

H.M.S.O.   *Coastal Command. The Air Ministry Account of the Part Played by Coastal Command in the Battle of the Seas 1939 – 1942* (London, 1942).

Hobsbawm, Eric   *The Forward March of Labour Halted? Marxism Today* (London, 1978).

Horrall, Andrew — *Popular Culture in London c. 1890-1918. The Transformation of Entertainment* (Manchester, 2001).

Howarth, Ken — *Oral History* (Stroud, 1999).

Howes, S.D. — *Goosepool. The History of RAF and RCAF Middleton St. George and Teesside Airport* (Darlington, 2003).

Humphries, S. — *Hooligans or Rebels? An Oral History of Working-Class Childhood 1889-1939*, (London, 1981).

Hunt, Leslie — *Twenty-one Squadrons. The History of the Royal Auxiliary Air Force 1925-1957* (London, 1972).

Jackson, Alan A. — *The Middle Classes 1900 – 1950* (Nairn Scotland, 1991).

James, John — *The Paladins. A Social History of the outbreak of World War II* (London, 1990).

James, Lawrence — *The Middle Class. A History* (London, 2006.)

Janowitz, Morris — *The Professional Soldier. A Social and Political Portrait* (USA, 1960).

Jewell, Helen M. — *The North-South Divide. The Origins of Northern Consciousness in England* (Manchester, 1994).

Joyce, Patrick (ed), — *Class* (Oxford, 1995).

Kaye, Harvey J. — *The British Historians. An Introductory Analysis* (Cambridge, 1984).

Kennedy, Paul — *The Realities Behind Diplomacy. Background Influences on British External Policy 1865 – 1980* (London, 1981).

Kennedy, Paul — *The Rise and Fall of British Naval Mastery* (London, 1983 & 2004).

Kenny, Michael — *The First New Left. British Intellectuals After Stalin* (London, 1995).

Kidd, Alan & — *Gender, Civic Culture and* Nicholls, David (eds) *Consumerism. Middle Class Identity in Britain 1800 – 1940* (Manchester, 1999).

Kidd, Alan &
Nicholls, David (eds)

The Making of the British Middle Class. Studies of Regional and Cultural Diversity Since the Eighteenth Century (Stroud, 1998).

Koss, Stephen E.

Lord Haldane : Scapegoat for Liberalism (USA, 1969).

Lawton, Richard (ed)

The Census and Social Structure. An Interpretative Guide to 19th Century Censuses for England and Wales (London, 1978)

Leahy, William H., McKee, David L., & Dean, Robert D.

Urban Economics (New York, 1992).

Leonard, J.W.

Constantine College (Middlesbrough, 1981)

Louis, W.M. Roger &
Owen, Roger (eds)

Suez 1956. The Crisis and its Consequences (Oxford,1991)

Lucas, Laddie (ed)

Voices in the Air 1939-1945. Incredible stories of the World War II Airmen in Their Own Words (London, 2003).

Lummis, Trevor

Listening to History (London, 1987).

Mackay, James

Collecting Local History (London, 1984).

Mackay, Robert

Half the battle. Civilian Morale in Britain during the Second World War (Manchester, 2002).

McKenzie, John M.

Imperialism and Popular Culture (Manchester, 1986).

MacKenzie, S.P.

The Home Guard – A Military and Political History (Oxford, 1996).

McKibbin, Ross

Classes and Cultures. England 1918-1950 (Oxford, 1998).

McKibbin, Ross

The Ideologies of Class. Social Relations in Britain 1880-1950 (Oxford, 1990).

Marwick, Arthur

Britain in the Century of Total War. War, Peace and Social Change 1900-1967, (Harmondsworth, 1968).

Marwick, Arthur (ed)

Total War and Social Change (London, 1988).

Millin, Sarah Gertrude

General Smuts (London, 1976).

Morris, R.J.

Class, Sect and Party. The Making of the British Middle Class. Leeds 1820 – 1850 (Manchester, 1990).

Morris, Robert J. & Trainer, Richard H. (eds)	*Urban Governance. Britain and Beyond Since 1750* (Aldershot, 1998).
Moulson, Tom	*The Flying Sword. The Story of 601 Squadron* (London, 1964).
Mowat, Charles Loch	*Britain Between the Wars 1918 – 1940* (London, 1955).
Murray, W.	*War in the Air 1914 – 1945* (London, 1999).
Nesbitt, Roy Conyers	*Coastal Command in Action 1939 – 1945* (Gloucestershire, 1997).
Nesbitt, Roy Conyers	*An Illustrated History of the RAF* (Surrey, 1990).
Newton, Tony	*Pins and Needles and Paperclips: Treasures from the Royal Aero Club Archives* (London, 2006).
Nicholas, Katherine	*The Social Effects of Unemployment in Teesside* (Manchester, 1986).
Norman, B	*Wartime Teesside* (Lancaster, 1989).
Norris, Andrew	*Reminiscence with Elderly People* (Bicester Oxon., 1986).
North, G.A.	*Teesside's Economic Heritage* (Cleveland, 1975).
Obelkevich, James & Catterall, Peter (eds)	*Understanding Post-War British Society* (London, 1994).
O'Connell, Sean	*The Car in British Society. Class, Gender and Motoring 1896 – 1939* (Manchester, 1998).
Omissi, David E.	*Air Power and Colonial Control. The Royal Air Force 1919 – 1939* (Manchester, 1960).
Onderwater, Hans	*"Gentlemen in Blue". 600 Squadron* (Barnsley, 1997).
Ottler, Patrick	*Yorkshire Airfields in the Second World War* (Newbury 1998).
Owens, Francis Gerard	*Winds of Change – Stockton on Tees 1800-1939* (Stockton on Tees, 1990).
Panichas, George A. (ed)	*Promise of Greatness. The War of 1914 – 1918* (London, 1968).

Parker, M.
The Battle of Britain July – October 1940. An Oral History of Britain's 'Finest Hour' (London, 2000).

Parker, R.A.C.
Chamberlain and Appeasement. British Policy and the Coming of the Second World War (London,1993)

Pearce, I.
Lost on Easby Moor. The Last Flight of Hudson NR -E (Wolviston, 2003).

Peden, G.C.
British Rearmament and the Treasury 1932 – 1939 (Edinburgh, 1979).

Perkin, Harold
The Rise of Professional Society. England since 1880 (London, 1989).

Piper, Ian
We Never Slept. The History of 605 (County of Warwick) Squadron Royal Auxiliary Air Force 1926 – 1957 (Tamworth, 1996).

Pollard, A.J. (ed)
Middlesbrough – Town and County 1830 – 1950 (Stroud, 1996)

Powell, W.W. (ed)
The Non-Profit Sector, A Research Handbook (New Haven 1987).

Powers, Barry D.
Strategy without Slide Rule. British Air Strategy 1914-1939 (London, 1976).

Price, Mary
The Photograph: A Strange Confined Space (Stanford University, 1994).

Price, R.
An Imperial War and the British Working Class. Attitudes and Reactions to the Boer War 1899 - 1902 (Toronto, 1972).

Rawlings, John D.R.
The History of the Royal Air Force (Feltham,1984).

Reader, W.J.
At Duty's Call – A Study in Obsolete Patriotism (Manchester, 1988).

Reader, W.J.
Imperial Chemical Industries. A History. Volume 2. The First Quarter Century 1926 - 1952 (London, 1975).

Reader, W.J.
Professional Men. The Rise of the Professional Classes in Nineteenth Century England (London, 1966).

Reid, Alastair J.
Social Classes and Social Relations in Britain 1850 – 1914 (Basingstoke, 1992).

Richards, Denis — *Royal Air Force 1939 – 1945, Volume 1 – The Fight at Odds* (London, 1974).

Richardson, Dick — *The Evolution of British Disarmament Policy in the 1920s* (London, 1989).

Richardson, Joy — *Looking at Local Records* (London, 1983).

Rider, Philip — *Local History – A Handbook for Beginners* (London, 1983).

Rock, William R. — *British Appeasement in the 1930s* (London, 1977).

Ross, Tony — *75 Eventful Years. A Tribute to the Royal Air Force 1918 – 1993* (London, 1993).

Royal Air Force Historical Society — *Royal Air Force Reserve and Auxiliary Forces* (Oxford, 2003).

Royal Air Force Volunteer Reserve — *Memories* (Gloucester, 1997).

Royle, Edward — *Modern Britain. A Social History 1750-1997* (London, 1987).

Rubinstein, W.D. — *Capitalism, Culture and Decline in Britain 1750 – 1990* (London, 1994).

Samuel, Raphael (ed) — *Patriotism. The Making and Unmaking of British National Identity. Volume 1 History and Politics* (London, 1989)

Samuel, Raphael (ed) — Patriotism. The Making and Unmaking of British National Identity, Volume 2 Minorities and Outsiders (London, 1989)

Samuel, Raphael (ed) — Patriotism. The Making and Unmaking of British National Identity, Volume 3 national Fictions (London, 1989)

Schmidt, Gustav — *The Politics and Economics of Appeasement. British Foreign Policy in the 1930s* (Leamington Spa, 1986).

Scott, W.H., Banks, J.A., Halsey, A.H. & Lupton, T. — *Technical Change and Industrial Relations. A Study of the Relations between Technical Change and the Social Structuring of a Large Steelworks* (Liverpool, 1956).

Seldon, Anthony & Pappworth, Joanna — *By Word of Mouth. Elite Oral History* (London,1983).

Sharp, Thomas — *Town and Countryside. Some Aspects of Urban and Rural Development* (London, 1932).

Sharpe, M. — *History of the Royal Air Force* (London, 1999).

Smith, David J. — *Britain's Military Airfields 1939 – 1945* (Yeovil Somerset, 1989).

Smith, H. L. (Ed) — *War and Social change. British Society in the Second World War* (Manchester, 1986).

Smith, Harold — *Britain in the Second World War. A Social History* (Manchester, 1996).

Smith, Malcolm — *British Air Strategy Between the Wars* (Oxford, 1984).

Smithies, Edward — *Aces, Erks and Backroom Boys. Aircrew, Ground Staff and Warplane Builders Remember the Second World War* (London, 2002).

Smuts, J.C. — *Jan Christian Smuts* (London, 1952).

Sockett, E.W. — *608 Squadron and RAF Thornaby* (Middlesbrough, 1975).

Steel, Nigel & Hart, Peter — *Tumult in the Clouds. The British Experience of the War in the Air 1914 – 1918* (London, 1997).

Stevens, J.R. — *Searching for the Hudson Bombers. Lads, Love and Death in World War II* (Victoria, 2004).

Stevenson, John — *British Society 1914 – 1945* (London, 1984).

Stevenson, John — *The Pelican Social History of Britain. British Society 1914 – 1945* (London, 1984).

Taylor, A.J.P. — *English History 1914 – 1945* (Oxford 1965).

Tedder, The Lord G.C.B. — *Air Power in War – The Lees Knowles Lectures by Marshal of the Royal Air Force* (London, 1947).

Thomas, Hugh — *The Suez Affair* (Harmondsworth Middlesex, 1967).

Thompson, E.P. — *The Making of the English Working Class* (London, 1963).

Thompson, F.M.L. (ed) — *The Cambridge Social History of Britain 1750-1950, Volume 2, People and their Environment* (Cambridge, 1990).

Thompson, F.M.L. (ed) — The Cambridge Social History of Britain 1750-1950, Volume 3 Social Agencies and Institutions (Cambridge, 1990)

Thompson, Neville — *The Anti-Appeasers. Conservative Opposition to Appeasement in the 1930s* (London, 1971).

Thompson, Paul — *The Voice of the Past. Oral History* (Oxford, 2000).

Tiratsoo, Nick (ed) — *From Blitz to Blair. New Labour and its Past* (London, 1997).

Titmuss, Richard — *Problems of Social Policy* (London, 1950).

Tosh, John — *The Pursuit of History* (London, 2000).

Turner, John — *MacMillan* (London, 1994).

Waites, Bernard — *A Class Society at War. England 1914 – 1918* (Leamington Spa, 1987).

Watkins, David — *Fear Nothing. The History of No. 501 (County of Gloucester) Fighter Squadron, Royal Auxiliary Air Force* (Cowden Kent, 1990).

Weight, Richard & Beach, Abigail (eds) — *The Right to Belong. Citizenship and National Identity in Britain 1930 – 1960* (London, 1998).

Weisbrod, B.A. — *The Non Profit Economy* (Cambridge Massachusetts, 1988).

Wellum, G — *First Light* (London, 2003).

White, Ian — *If you want Peace, Prepare for War. A History of No 604 (County of Middlesex) Squadron, RauxAF, in Peace and in War* (London, 2005).

Wiener, Martin J. — *English Culture and the Decline of the Industrial Spirit 1850 – 1980* (Cambridge, 2004).

Williams, Raymond — *Keywords – A Vocabulary of Culture and Society* (London, 1976).

Willmott, P. & Young, M. — *Family and Class in a London Suburb* (London, 1960).

Wilson, Keith M,   *Empire and Continent – Studies in British Foreign Policy from the 1880s to the First World War* (London, 1987).

Wright, Richard   *Patriots. National Identity in Britain 1940 – 2000* (London, 2002).

Young, Michael   *The Rise of the Meritocracy* (London, 1994).

Yow, Valerie Raleigh   *Recording Oral History. A Practical Guide for Social Scientists* (London, 1994).

Ziegler, F.H.   *The Story of 609 Squadron. Under the White Rose* (London, 1971).

Journals

Blanche, B.   'Weekend Fliers', *Aeroplane* 27, 8 (1999).

Boswell, Jonathan   'The Informal Social Control of Business In Britain 1980 – 1939', *Business History Review* 57, 2 (1983).

Bowyer, M.J.F.   'Royal Auxiliary Air Force'. *Scale Aircraft Modelling* 7, 1 (1984).

Crowson, N.J.   'Contemporary Record', *The Conservative Party and the Call for National Service, 1937 – 1939: Compulsion Versus Voluntarism* 9, 1 (1995).

Dewey, P.E.   'Military Recruiting and the British Labour Force during the First World War', *The History Journal*, 27, 1 (1984).

Douglas, R.   'Voluntary Enlistment in the First World War and the Work of the Parliamentary Recruiting Committee' *Journal of Modern History* 4, (1970).

Farr, Martin   'A Compelling Case for Voluntarism: Britain's Alternative Strategy 1915 – 1916', *War in History* 9, 2 (2002).

Finlayson, G.   'A Moving Frontier – Voluntarism and the State in British Social Welfare', *Twentieth Century British History* 1, 2 (1990).

Gunn, Simon   'Class Identity and the Urban: the Middle Class in England c. 1790 – 1950', *Urban History* 31, 1 (2004).

Harris, Jose   'Political Thought and the Welfare State 1870-1914: An Intellectual Framework for British Social Policy', *Past and Present* 135 (1992),

Hartigan, J.   'Volunteering for the Army in England. August 1914 – May 1915' *Midland History* 24 (1999).

Hinton, James   'Middle-class Socialism: Selfhood, Democracy and Distinction in Wartime County Durham', *History Workshop Journal* 62.

Mansell, Dr. A.   'Professionals, Amateurs and Private Armies. Pilot Entry Portals in the RAF Expansion of 1934 to 1939', *Proceedings of the RAF Historical Society* 11 (1993).

Mansell, Tony   'Flying Start: Educational and Social Factors in the Recruitment of Pilots of the Royal Air Force in the Inter-War Years' *History of Education* 26, No. 1, (1997).

Paris, M. 'The Rise of the Airmen: The Origins of Airforce Elitism c. 1890 – 1918', *Journal of Contemporary History* 28 (1993).

Petler, Martin   '"Temporary Gentlemen" in the aftermath of the Great War: Rank, Status and the Ex-officer Problem', *The Historical Journal* 37, 1 (1994).

Rieger, B.   'Fast Couples: Technology and Modernity in Britian and Germany during the Nineteen-Thirties', *Historical Research* 76, 193 (2003).

Russell, Dave   'The Heaton Review 1927 – 1934: Culture, Class and a Sense of Place in Interwar Yorkshire', *Twentieth Century British History* 17, 3 (2006).

Saler, Michael   'Making it New: Modernism and the "Myth of the North" in Interwar England', *Journal of British Studies* 37 (1998).

Samuel, Raphael   'Middle Class Between the Wars (Parts 1 and 2)', *New Socialist* (1983).

Samuel, Raphael   'Suburbs Under Siege. The Middle Class Between the Wars (Part 3)', *New Socialist* (1983).

Smith, J   'Urban Elites c. 1830 – 1930 and Urban History', *Urban History* 27, 2 (2000).

Collections

Banks, J.A.

'The Social Structure of Nineteenth Century England as seen through the Census, Chapter 6, P 179 – 224' in Richard Lawton (ed) *The Census and Social Structure. An Interpretative Guide to 19th Century Censuses for England and Wales* (London,1978).

Briggs, Asa

'Middlesbrough:The Growth of a New Community, Chapter 1, p. 2-7' in A. J. Pollard (ed), *Middlesbrough Town and Community 1830-1950*, (Stroud, 1996).

Cunningham, H.

'Leisure and Culture, Chapter 6, p279-341' in F.M.L. Thompson *Cambridge Social History*, 2 (Cambridge, 1990).

Fielding, Steven

'The Good War', in Nick Tiratsoo (ed) *From Blitz to Blair. New Labour and its Past*, (London, 1997).

Freeman, Squadron Leader A.F.

'The Post-War Royal Auxiliary Air Force' in Royal Air Force Historical Society *Royal Air Force Reserve and Auxiliary Forces* (Oxford, 2003).

Jefford, Jeff

'Post-War Reserves to 1960' in Royal Air Force Historical Society *Royal Air Force Reserve and Auxiliary Forces* (Oxford, 2003).

Hansmann, H.

'Economic Theories of Non-Profit Organisations' in *W.W. Powell (Ed) The Non Profit Sector, A Research Handbook* (1987).

Harris, Jose

'Society and the State in 20th Century Britain, Chapter 3, p. 63 – 117 in F.M.L. Thompson *The Cambridge Social History of Britain 1750 – 1900, Vol 3, Social Agencies and Institutions* (Cambridge, 1990).

Law, Christopher M.

'Employment and Industrial Structure' in James Obelkevich and Peter Catterall *Understanding Post-War British Society* (London, 1994).

Lewis, Jane

'The Voluntary Sector in The Mixed Economy of Welfare, Introduction Page 4.' in David Gladstone (Ed) *Before Beveridge, Welfare before the Welfare State, Civitas Choice in Welfare* 47 (London, 1999).

Mansell, Dr. Tony	'Royal Air Force Volunteer Reserve 1936 – 1939' in Royal Air Force Historial Society *Royal Air Force Reserve and Auxiliary Forces (Oxford, 2003).*
Morris, R.J.	'Clubs, Societies and Associations, Chapter 8, p.395 – 443' in F.M.L. Thompson *Cambridge Social History* 3, (Cambridge, 1990).
Salamon, L.M.	'Partners in Public Service. The Scope and Theory of Government; Non Profit Relations' in W.W. Powell (ed) *The Non Profit Sector. A Research Handbook* (New Haven, 1987).
Seed, John	'"Middling Sort" in Late 18th Century and Early 19th Century England' in M.L. Bush (ed) *Social Orders and Social Classes in Europe Since 1500* (Harlow, 1992).
Shores, Christopher	'The Auxiliary Air Force in W W II' in Royal Air Force Historical Society *Royal Air Force Reserve and Auxiliary Forces* (Oxford 2003).
Summerfield, P.	'The Levelling of Class' in H. L. Smith (ed) *War and Social Change. British Society in the Second World War*, (Manchester, 1986).
Thane, P.	'Government and Society in England and Wales 1750-1914' in F. M. L. Thompson (ed), *The Cambridge Social History of Britain,* Page 1. (Cambridge 1919).

Theses

Williamson, Margaret

'Partnership and Power: The Organisation of Gender Roles in the East Cleveland Mining Communities 1918-1964 (PhD Thesis: University of Teesside, 1997).

Web Addresses

Morris, Suzannah

'Social Policy from the Victorians to the Present day, Voluntary Provision in a Mixed Economy. (The London School of Economics and Political Science.) [www.fathom.com/course/21701744/index.html], 18th May 2006.

Air Ministry

Series Details: Air Ministry and Successors: Operations Record Books, Squadrons, 1911 – 1972. [www.nationalarchives.gov.uk]

Round Table

'About Roundtable' Origins
www.roundtable.co.uk/about/phb

Charles Gambier Jenyns

www.rogerco.freeserve.co.uk/

Jack Elkan David Benham

www.roll-of-honour.com/
www.uk-cigars.co.uk

William Henry Rhodes-Moorhouse

www.carpages.co.uk/news

Arthur Hammond Dalton

www.cwgc.org/search

Edward Lawrence Colbeck-Welch

www.kcl.ac.uk

Peter Kenneth Devitt

www.hyderabad.co.uk

Anthony Henry Hamilton Tollemache

www.ww2awards.com

Paul Richey

www.bbc..co.uk/history

Geoffrey Ambler

www.rafweb.org//biographies

Kenneth Maxwell Stoddart

www.bowringpark.co.uk

Various AAF officers

www.thepeerage.com

Walter Leslie Runciman&
Lancelot Eustace Smith

www.norav.50megs.com

Cecil Leonard Knox

www.remuseum.org

Various AAF officers

http://en.wikipedia.org

Map of Teesside Area

www.yellowtom.co.uk/Teesside/map

Thornaby Aerodrome
Ground Plans
Map of England
RAF Air Bases in England

http://hammer.prohosting.com/Thornaby
www.worldatlas.com
www.anti-aircraft.co.uk/airfieldmap

INDEX